FREDERICK ASHTON

Sir FREDERICK ASHTON, C.H., C.B.E.,
Director of the Royal Ballet 1963–1970, and its Founder Choreographer

FREDERICK ASHTON

A CHOREOGRAPHER AND HIS BALLETS

ZOË DOMINIC
JOHN SELWYN GILBERT

GEORGE G. HARRAP & COMPANY LIMITED
LONDON   TORONTO   WELLINGTON   SYDNEY

Layout: Ann Gilbert

Black and white prints: Bryan Hall, Robert Horner

Jacket print: Derek Manchee

For photographs on pages 33, 54, 122 we are indebted
to John Hayes and the London Museum, Mary Clarke
and *The Dancing Times*, and G. B. L. Wilson

First published in Great Britain 1971
by GEORGE G. HARRAP & CO. LTD
182–184 High Holborn, London, WC1V 7AX

Standard edn. ISBN 0 245 50351 X
Limited edn. ISBN 0 245 50571 7

Composed in Bodoni type and Printed by
JARROLD & SONS LTD, Norwich

Made in Great Britain

PREFACE

Of all the contemporary choreographers, Frederick Ashton is the most widely accomplished. He has created almost all the possible types of ballet and he has largely manufactured the English style of dancing, classical, lyrical, gentle, beautiful feet and weak backs as the Russians unkindly put it when they first saw the Royal Ballet. Ashton's career has been so long and distinguished, as well as interesting, that it's extraordinary that so few books have been devoted to him or deal with him at length. It's very gratifying to be among the first to pay him tribute.

Our original intention, more than two years ago, was to make a book that would combine our admiration for Ashton's work, our fond affection for the man himself and our respect for his enormous, varied, colourful contribution to the history of British ballet. This, in the end, is roughly what we've done though we have also tried to make the book into a serious study—sometimes critical but never, unhappily, quite comprehensive—of Ashton's career, and some of his ballets and the causes and effects of his having created them. This book is not, of course, the authoritative assessment of Ashton's work as a choreographer which his achievements have merited. That still remains to be written. But even when it is, perhaps our book will prove useful and entertaining. Ashton's personal wit and charm should also be reflected in the pages that follow, just as they illuminate and are reflected in his choreography. We owe an enormous debt to him.

ZOË DOMINIC
JOHN SELWYN GILBERT

ACKNOWLEDGEMENTS

This book would not have been written if the colleagues and friends of Frederick Ashton had not given time and energy to make it possible. It is based on interviews with Cecil Beaton, William Chappell, Dame Margot Fonteyn, Alexander Grant, Sir Robert Helpmann, Dame Marie Rambert, Michael Somes, and Dame Ninette de Valois. I was also able to quote from correspondence with Bronislava Nijinska and to use passages from interviews with the cast of Ashton's ENIGMA VARIATIONS, the text of which was made available by Harley Usill of the Argo Record Company. Ian Horsbrugh allowed me to look at interview material which he had gathered for a B.B.C. programme about Ashton and Clive Barnes' essay on Ashton (Dance Perspectives, 1961, reprinted by the Johnson Reprint Corporation in 1970), and Mary Clarke's books (*The Sadler's Wells Ballet*—A. and C. Black, 1955; *Dancers of Mercury*—A. and C. Black, 1962) were of particular importance to me. I also consulted many books and articles by Arnold Haskell and C. W. Beaumont and many copies of *Ballet, Dance and Dancers* and *The Dancing Times*. A brief quotation from Walter Sorrell's *The Dance has Many Faces* appears on page 164.

In addition we would like to thank: The Archivist of the Royal Opera House, Covent Garden, David Aukin, for reading and criticizing the manuscript at all stages, William Bainbridge, of George G. Harrap & Company Ltd., Richard Buckle and Edwin Denby for permission to quote from *Ballet*, Janis Gamgee, for transcribing tape-recorded interviews and notes, Irina Kirillova, for translating to and from Russian, Sheila Porter, for information and all sorts of assistance, Edith Russell Roberts (née Edith Ashton), Hilary Rubinstein, of A. P. Watt & Son, and Sarah Spare, for secretarial help and research.

CONTENTS

"We met Fred Ashton. I am always asking Alice Toklas do you think he is a genius, she does have something happen when he is a genius, so I always ask her is he a genius, being one it is natural that I should think a great deal about that thing in any other one.

"He and I talked about a great deal on meeting, and I think he is one. More likely than any one we have seen for a long time. He was born in Peru and was for three years when a young boy in a monastery and his parents were both English but he does know what it is to be a Peruvian and that made it possible for him to do what he did with FOUR SAINTS to make a religious procession sway and slowly disappear without moving, perhaps being a Peruvian will help him with THE WEDDING BOUQUET."

GERTRUDE STEIN

(from Everybody's Autobiography)
quoted by Beryl de Zoete in an essay
which first appeared in HORIZON in 1942

"Frederick Ashton has a great genius, and what's so damned irritating is that it's impossible to put your finger on it and find out what it consists of. If only one could, one could try and get it for oneself."

MICHAEL SOMES

"At the beginning of June, 1928, when I was recruiting for the Ballets Ida Rubinstein, I received a letter from Frederick Ashton asking for an audition. He concluded his letter 'si vous décidez de m'appeler à votre service, je travaillerai de tout cœur,' and he kept that promise to the full. From Ashton's first days with the company his serious attitude to his work and his enthusiasm were obvious. He was not completely ready for classical dancing, but in character dances he was among the best. He stood out by his exact rendering of style and his flawless accuracy in the details of my choreography. Ashton did not dance solo parts when he was with the Ballets Ida Rubinstein, but he knew how to render individual what he did in ensembles.

"In addition, as his colleagues told me, he had a unique gift for mimicry—he could mimic every artist in the company, Ida Rubinstein, myself, Wiltzak, Schollar, Nikolaeva and others. He had a talent for noticing every trait, every line of the body, the rhythm of a person's movement and so on. These are qualities which every choreographer should possess. I myself did not see his imitations, but he kept his fellow dancers laughing and I can readily believe that he used to do them. He was always very witty and he knew how to inject an element of satire into his imitations. He was also very musical."

BRONISLAVA NIJINSKA (California 1970)

opposite and following: Frederick Ashton and Robert Helpmann as the Ugly Sisters in CINDERELLA

"Of course I've danced with Fred. Before the war I danced with him in LES SYLPHIDES and in NOCTURNE and in some other ballets. I think he was completely engrossed in what he was doing. He was terribly happy to be on stage; it was what he really loved. I once said to him that a choreographer I don't admire was 'just a frustrated dancer'. And Fred replied 'But we're all frustrated dancers.' He seemed rather surprised at the idea that anyone who could be a really good dancer would bother to become a choreographer."

MARGOT FONTEYN

"One never thought of Fred, at least I never did, as having a career as a dancer. He had quite a serious and hard-working life as a dancer which must have given him his enormous feeling for movement, but I only saw him as a choreographer."

NINETTE DE VALOIS

"I think that he is absolutely a born choreographer, pre-destined by God to do choreography. He has all the qualities, the eye, the judgment, an instinct for movement and musicality, besides which he has a lot of culture and an enormous amount of taste. What more could you want? In addition, he is extremely intelligent, he knows where to go and look for his material and he was always more prepared to work on choreography than dancing. He was inflamed by it. He got other people to do his dancing for him once he became a choreographer."

MARIE RAMBERT

Frederick William Mallandaine Ashton, doyen of British choreographers, lives in a very tiny, rather cold, house in Chelsea. He has lived there for some years, and the house is very typical of the man. The main room is curiously shaped and crowded, a sitting-room and study that is also almost a vestibule, and his favourite armchair faces into this room, away from French windows that open into a minute paved garden where he grows roses and sometimes camellias. The room is crammed with furniture, pictures and ornaments. The mantelpiece holds invitations and a portrait by Cecil Beaton. It is all both characteristic and 'comme il faut'. It is very English, a little mannered, very cosy. When I visit him a table is brought in to hold my tape recorder.

Although nothing in Frederick Ashton's manner now suggests it, he wasn't born or wholly brought up in England. Instead, he was born in Guayaquil in Ecuador on 17 September 1904. His father, it appears, had settled in South America in the 1890's and made his life there. Ashton's mother eloped to join him in 1895, the year they married. But relatively little is known of Ashton's family or his very early life. Even his date of birth is often, and mistakenly, said to be 1906. Ashton's own account of his life as a child, at school, and before he became successful as a dancer, has never previously been published.   J.S.G.

FREDERICK ASHTON IN CONVERSATION

FAMILY AND EARLY LIFE

"I think," says Frederick Ashton, "that when my mother married it was really rather a question of 'anything to get away from Suffolk', which was where she lived; because, you see, my mother was a very spirited woman and immensely alive and humorous and witty. She had a great zest for life and any talent that I have comes out of her.

"My father was very different, and I don't think that my parents were ever very happy together—I seem to remember that part of it quite clearly. After meals my mother sat in one room and he sat in another and my mother was very socially inclined. I never saw too much of her when I was young.

"Of course I was a babe in arms when we left Ecuador, where I was born. All I remember of South America is Lima, in Peru, where we lived until I came to England. My father was a sort of honorary consul in Lima and I think he worked for a cable company as well but we were really just a rather large middle-class family. I had three elder brothers and a step-brother, then, finally, a younger sister.

"I was always terrified of my father when I was young. I don't know why now except that he used to make me eat things I couldn't manage. I steered clear of him as much as I could and I remember him as short with a large nose and blue eyes, a rather severe man, withdrawn into himself and with a very strong melancholic streak which I think I inherited. I was always terrified of him and he was very strict indeed with me, though he was also incredibly generous and any English beachcomber who told him a reasonable story was in the house before we knew it, dossing down. He had some property on the outskirts of Lima, in a slum, and he was a kind of hero there, because he built better houses. All the people came out to greet him when he walked past. As a matter of fact he spent an enormous amount of his time out there because he had a walled garden where he grew nothing but carnations.

"Of course as a child in that sort of household I spent my time mostly with the servants and with the people who looked after me. All the people I played with were Peruvians, and I spoke more Spanish than English when I was young. Although we were supposed to be English boys and there was an English colony in Lima I never thought of England at all. It never entered my head."

SCHOOL

"When I was about eight, just after my sister was born, I started to go to school. It was a Dominican school in Lima and all I can remember learning there is how to pray. I spent an enormous amount of time in church and I was even prepared for my first communion, only my mother found out and that was stopped. But although I wasn't a Catholic I still used to assist at all the Masses in Lima cathedral. I was the favourite acolyte of the Archbishop of Lima because I was blond.

"At that time there were only two real schools in Lima, one run by the Jesuits and one by the Dominicans. They were the Eton and Harrow of education in Lima but at the one where I went everything was done in French because the priests were French. It was a very long hard day for a boy, from 8.30 or 9.00 in the morning right through till 5. When I was about thirteen the English Minister in Lima started a school, and so I was taken away from the Dominicans and sent there instead."

PAVLOVA

"At about this time my father went back to Ecuador because of his business and I went to live in a place called Miraflores with a family. Then, when Pavlova came round on one of her tours, I went with the Watson family to see her. It was the first time I'd been to a ballet and the first time I'd been in a motor car also, and Guy Watson, who was about my age, was only interested in the car and longed for the performance to finish so that he could get back into it for the drive home. I didn't care about that but I can still remember that Pavlova danced FAIRY DOLL at that performance. When the curtains parted she was in a sort of booth, just standing there, and I thought she was terribly ugly because she was rather beaky and seemed very old. But when she danced I thought she was quite, quite beautiful. Seeing her at that stage was the end of me. She injected me with her poison and from the end of that evening I wanted to dance. Coming from middle-class parents it was a horrifying thought.

"The thing about Pavlova that I remember is that she had an enormous personality and an enormous impact on an audience. She excited us—she brought people to their feet. And then she had extraordinary grace and plasticity and her performances were always very vivid. No one who saw her has forgotten her. My mother went backstage to be introduced to her during that season in Lima, and I caught a glimpse of her in the street outside the theatre. I was also told that she went to 'thé dansants', which they used to have in those days, and spotted my eldest brother, who was a most beautiful ballroom dancer, and asked him to join her company. He was horrified and absolutely shocked and refused point blank. It was unthinkable."

DOVER COLLEGE

"In 1919, when the First World War was over, I was sent back to England from South America with the Watsons and I started at public school. I went to Dover College. My mother was a friend of the Headmaster of Clifton School, he recommended me to Dover, and I got in on the strength of that. Because, you see, I would never have been able to pass any entrance exam. I didn't know the rudiments of anything, or even how to learn. There's someone I still see who always reminds me that when we'd just arrived at Dover a master told us to open our algebra books and I turned to him—at least that is what he says—and asked 'What is algebra, anyway?'

"I must say that my schooldays were an absolute desert for me. Guy Watson went to Dover at the same time, and fitted in perfectly but unless you were good at games, which I wasn't, it was all quite hopeless. There was the ghastly English climate and the change from South America, and I even spoke English with a Spanish accent when I arrived at Dover. We were terribly ill-treated as new boys. Nowadays one would just walk out of the school but in my generation we were disciplined. I was brought up to be seen and not heard, even by my father, so I suffered it as something ghastly that had to be gone through. I accepted the jungle law. I cheated my way through and cribbed from other people and in the end I did make friends. But it turned me very much into myself, and I think I used to write my mother very pathetic letters. I remember that when she came down to see the Headmaster at one stage she told me that I was being 'mawkish', whatever that means. Even my mother was quite aloof, you see. There wasn't this idea of knowing and sympathizing with your children and I would never have dared to tell my father about school or complain to him. He wouldn't have listened."

THE THEATRE

"At this time, because my parents were still living in South America, I was billeted during the holidays with an old school friend of my mother. She had a tiny flat in the King's Road, Chelsea, and I used to have to play cribbage with her aged mother most evenings. There was nothing else to do.

"At first it was all rather unfortunate because I used to rush back from school for the holidays, longing to go to theatres and concerts, and she didn't think that was right for a boy. She used to carry me off to the country somewhere and when we were in town she locked me in at 10.30 every night. So I was only ever in London for short periods, say ten days, and I used to go to twelve or fifteen theatres. I'd go from a matinée straight on to an evening performance, because I sustained myself in that way; by reading, a certain amount but not a great deal; by listening to music and going to Promenade concerts; by theatre-going and also by visiting museums. Museums are a great outlet for the poor. It's somewhere to go and sit and look and be warm.

"The first ballet I saw after Pavlova was in 1921, when my parents came from South America to bring my sister back to school. I went to see Diaghilev's SLEEPING PRINCESS, which was quite terrific. I can still remember Spessitseva coming on in the Rose Adagio and I remember the Hunting Scene, because they had tremendous costumes, and after that I used to go to all the seasons at the Coliseum and I saw Pavlova again at Covent Garden. But the first real Diaghilev ballet I saw was LE TRAIN BLEU, which was the last word in modernity, and then LES BICHES and L'APRÉS-MIDI D'UN FAUNE and LES NOCES much later, the night before we opened in TRAGEDY OF FASHION. I remember the audience reaction was very strange, rather hostile to LES NOCES. But I was excited by it."

THE CITY

"At school, because I had the most marvellous capacity for not learning anything that didn't interest me, I could never pass exams. So when I came to leave I was looked upon as a sort of hopeless character and pushed into the City instead of into the Diplomatic Service, which was what my mother wanted. Frankly, it was more shattering to be pushed into the City than almost anything else that ever happened to me. I started as an office boy with a firm of import-export merchants and I didn't mind that at all at first. I rather enjoyed the filing and licking the stamps. But my guardian's brother was a partner in this firm and so I was promoted and I had to do business and after that it became quite hopeless. I was what was known as a foreign correspondent. I used to translate business letters in any language and the manager would bring me letters in Arabic and I'd say 'But I don't speak Arabic' and he'd say 'But you speak Spanish. And there's a dictionary over there.' I was expected to translate any letter that came in.

"I must say I still don't know how I stood it in the City. It was all terribly restricted and frustrated and closed up. But my father had by this time committed suicide —he'd started his own business and I think it had gone wrong—and my mother came home to England after that and I had to keep her. So I was in the City for a year and a half."

MASSINE

"It was during this period, some time after my father died, that I began to take lessons with Massine. He put an advertisement in some paper and a school-friend called Reginald Palmer found this advertisement and showed it to me. I wrote to Massine and asked if I could have a trial lesson, which was what he had offered, and what should I wear? Eventually he wrote back telling me to wear soft slippers and pyjamas which, with my rigid upbringing, I didn't think was right at all. So I wore cricket flannels and a shirt.

"Of course I was terribly lucky to fall into the right hands from the start. I remember old Mrs Beaumont at the Ballet Bookshop saying 'You looked in *The Dancing Times*? Goodness, you might as well have looked into the telephone directory.' Massine was very aloof and uncommunicative and you couldn't get near him at all but he was interested in teaching because he wanted to form a troupe. There were about a dozen pupils in all, most of them rather arty girls. And all I remember is that after I'd done five or six classes I said 'Well, when you are going to teach me a dance?' and he said 'In three years time.' I was frightfully depressed about that. I hated classes.

"At first, because I was in the City, I was only able to go to Massine on Saturday afternoons. It cost me a guinea a week so that although I was earning thirty or thirty-five shillings a week I could never pay for anything, not even my washing. I never had a penny and when my mother came back from South America she couldn't understand why I had no money, because I didn't dare confess that I was taking ballet lessons. Only then I began to get terribly thin and really worried and I lost the firm £1,000 through misquoting the exchange rates and a marvellous old Scottish doctor was called in because I'd gone to bed and wouldn't get up. He was frightfully wise and he said 'There's nothing really wrong, but what's the matter?' So I told him about my dancing lessons and he told my mother that unless I was allowed to do ballet I might end in the loony-bin. That frightened her and then she thought she'd better concede. Which she did, though all my family were outraged and even she could never bring herself to tell anyone that I was dancing. She always said I'd 'gone on the stage' instead."

RAMBERT

"So we were all right for a little while and I began to go to Massine every day instead of just once a week. I think I learned a lot from him. I learned about style and about the beauty of 'port de bras', though he didn't teach me anything about choreography, not directly. As for the dancing, I always wanted to be the world's greatest dancer but I'd started much too late and I didn't have the physique to do it either. I wasn't at all strong technically and I got away with murder because there were very few dancers around. If I had to do it now I don't think I'd get far.

"Around the beginning of 1925 Massine left England for good and went back into the Diaghilev company. And he had already recommended me to Marie Rambert earlier than this, while he was working in Paris and on Cochran revues. So I went to Rambert again, although I must say that at first I didn't like her. Having come from Massine I wasn't sure that she had very much to offer. She only had a part-time studio in Bedford Gardens when I met her and she shared it with a lady sculptor who used to chase us out after about an hour. So I was always trying other teachers. I went to Legat at one period, and Rambert whisked me back, and I went to Astafieva and Margaret Craske when I could pay for lessons. Because with Rambert, although I paid her at one time, as soon as she knew I couldn't afford it she took me for nothing. That's why I kept coming back to her and eventually I became acclimatized, when I got to know her better.

"Of course Marie Rambert did contribute an enormous amount to my career because she's a remarkably intelligent woman, with an immense knowledge of literature and poetry and she influenced me tremendously in what I read—she cultivated me a great deal. I was always most aware of the intellectual qualities she had to offer and I was conscious that her analysis of things and her reasoning were very good. I wasn't nearly so aware of the musical side, although she did have Dalcroze training, but she certainly had a passion for dancing and she was extremely energetic and a great stimulus and it was in the early days with Rambert that I really started to get going."

ON STAGE

"In those days there used to be concerts given on the ends of piers. The agents used to book someone good for top of the bill and then fill in with anything, including me. My very first public performance was on the end of Brighton pier, but after that I appeared mainly in the charity matinées which Rambert did. And one of them involved Sophie Fedorovitch, who became my very closest friend.

"Sophie came to Rambert's class to draw us—that was my first sight of her—and I was terribly struck with the way she dressed. In those days everything was very conventional. But she wore masculine clothes, because she'd been through the Russian Revolution and she'd discarded all kinds of frippery. Everyone used to stare at her in the street. I was also struck by the beauty of her face, and she, as it turned out, was my Lilac Fairy. The greatest luck I ever had was meeting her.

"I worked with Sophie on my very first ballet, because she did the costumes.

She had a little studio on the Embankment, and she slept there and we worked there on A TRAGEDY OF FASHION in 1926. TRAGEDY was something we'd been asked to do by Nigel Playfair, who ran the Lyric, Hammersmith. He'd put on a revue called RIVERSIDE NIGHTS, which he'd also written, and the General Strike messed it up for him because no one could get to Hammersmith. So he moved it into the West End and then tried to move it back to the Lyric when the Strike was over. And he asked Rambert to do this ballet to help his revue along when it reopened. Which was very important for us, because there wasn't any ballet in those days and to be able to dance at all was rather a rarity."

A TRAGEDY OF FASHION

"I think the only thing for a choreographer is just to be in the right place at the right time and get down and do it. It's the only way you can see whether somebody has talent, I mean, you can't expect it to be perfect straight away but if someone shows some sort of spark—if there's a personal and individual style which comes across, a person's signature, even if it's really quite faint—then that's all right. Whether I had that in the beginning I don't know. I'm sure that A TRAGEDY OF FASHION was enormously derivative because my own part was influenced by Massine and in the girls' parts Nijinska's work for Diaghilev had influenced me also. But I dare say that in some ways it had something personal. It was a success, oddly enough. I was a couturier who stabbed himself with scarlet scissors because his collection wasn't satisfactory, and Marie Rambert was my partner, and it was to music by Eugene Goossens and he brought Diaghilev to see it—twice. I thought I was made for life. I thought the offers would come pouring in. But nothing happened.

"And of course that was the thing. There wasn't anything happening, and I kept trying to get away from it and do something serious. TRAGEDY ran for six weeks at the Lyric and I suppose I was paid ten pounds a week while it was on, but after that there was nothing. Because he'd seen the ballet, Diaghilev asked me to see him and audition for his company. But I felt so inadequate that I couldn't do it. I remember walking round and round the Lyceum Theatre and I couldn't go in because I was in a most terrible state. Knowing the standard of his company I felt I would have been hopeless, though afterwards I regretted not going very much. My mother asked me what he'd said and I made up something to tell her because I was ashamed of myself."

SOPHIE FEDOROVITCH

"Eventually, things went from bad to worse. There was no money at home and we were living in one room and my mother kept saying 'Oh well, you've tried it and you're not getting anywhere so now you must go back to the City and get a job.' And finally Sophie Fedorovitch had to persuade my mother to let me go on dancing. She got a friend to give my mother money, just so that I could. Rambert gave occasional evenings and charity performances and cocktail parties where there were ballets, and Diaghilev came to see us rehearse just before I went to the Rubinstein Company, in 1928. I remember that he asked me what I was doing and I told him and he gave me a sort of sardonic smile, because he disapproved of Rubinstein tremendously. But it didn't seem to me that he was interested in the ballets I'd done. So I borrowed money from Sophie to go to Paris and audition for Nijinska."

NIJINSKA

"The thing that a choreographer really needs is an eye. He has to do his training through his eye. It's not a thing you can teach, any more than you can teach people the rudiments of music and turn them into composers. I think that if someone has the desire to express himself in this way he should work under other choreographers. That's the only way I can see it happening, just like students did with Michelangelo and Raphael. I think that I learned to be a choreographer through watching other choreographers at work. And Nijinska, in particular, helped me tremendously. I never took my eyes off her when I was with Rubinstein. She reminded me once that at that stage I used to come and watch *all* her rehearsals, just to see her work. I used to sit in the corner all day long, just watching her.

"Of course Nijinska was extremely severe when we were rehearsing, a very hard taskmaster indeed. I remember once going to her because I was practically crippled. I couldn't move at all because her work was so difficult that my calves were completely seized up and so I asked if I could be let off rehearsals. And she said no—'C'est parce que vous n'avez pas l'habitude de travailler, ça passera.' I could have done myself a terrible harm, though I didn't. We were a very young company which she was trying to form and we were all terribly inexperienced and she just had to whip us into some kind of shape. You were at it all the time. There was no question of marking, you had to do everything full out. As a result, the standard of performance was extremely good. The company was recruited from all over the place, but it was always marvellously well rehearsed and all the 'corps de ballet' work was excellent. What let the company down was Ida Rubinstein herself. She took the leading roles and we used to build everything up for her and then she'd come on and the whole thing would collapse. I think we did twelve performances in the year I was with them and the same thing happened every time.

"Because both Billy Chappell and I were just ordinary members of the chorus in that company we practically starved to death together on the wages we were paid. We got 1000 francs a month, which was ten pounds, and so lunch could only cost six or seven francs and dinner eight or nine if you were going to manage; and you could never have a bath, because that was extra. I used to augment my money by giving English lessons to a Polish friend of Sophie's. But I can't imagine that I taught her much. I couldn't, and still can't, enlighten anyone on English grammar.

"When I left the Rubinstein company I didn't intend to leave it for good. I came back to England on holiday, and Rambert persuaded me to stay. But then Nijinska resigned and my contract lapsed, so there was no reason to go back. I think the whole thing collapsed and then revived much later."

IVY HOUSE

"I came back to England, I suppose, in the summer of 1929. Things were as quiet as before I left. The first ballet that I did was in a play by Ashley Dukes, and after that I did CAPRIOL SUITE.

"CAPRIOL SUITE was quite an important ballet for me, because it had music which I loved, by Peter Warlock, and it was done first at a Sunshine matinée at the Scala Theatre. Pavlova came to see it. She sat behind Arnold Haskell and apparently CAPRIOL was the only thing she was interested in. That's what he told me, though I think myself that she really came to see what Karsavina, who was dancing, was up to. But anyway, she asked Haskell about me and he told me that she'd asked and so I wrote to her next day and said that I'd like to hear her opinion. Victor Dandré replied and asked me to come to tea.

"As a dancer, Pavlova—and you must remember that she was my original inspiration —was very much a spirit and a flame, whereas Karsavina, who was her great rival, was a woman and a queen. In a very different way, Karsavina influenced me as much as Pavlova. But Karsavina's approach was much more reasoned and intellectual— Pavlova was all emotion and it was my memories of her which kept me going when I couldn't find work as a dancer and at school, when I was young, and when my mother and I had no money. So I went to Ivy House to see her in fear and trembling. Her first remark was 'Ach, so young,' and after that we had tea, and on the table there were lots and lots of little pots of jam from which she helped herself with enormous grace. We talked very freely and easily, and I was thrilled to meet her, but I was rather struck by her appearance, because she was getting on and her skin was like parchment and she looked very old to me. I was young enough then to think that everybody looked old.

"But I persuaded her to come and see more of my work at Rambert's—Arnold Haskell says that he persuaded her, but in fact I did it myself over that tea. She said that she couldn't, because she was about to go on tour. But, with great impetuosity, I said 'What time is your train? You could come on your way to the train.' She was rather taken aback, but she did it. She came and watched LEDA AND THE SWAN and a few snippets and she was very encouraging.

"After that I didn't see her again until the last matinée that she gave in England. I went to the theatre and asked to see her at the stage door. But the doorman said 'No, she doesn't see anyone after performances.' So I asked to see someone else I knew in the company. He let me in and of course I went straight to Pavlova's dressing room. Imagine the cheek! I banged on the door and Dandré let me in and I remember saying to myself, 'Notice her make-up' and 'Notice all the things about her.' But she had a scar, a sort of hole, on her breastbone—I think she'd stabbed herself during a ballet and the dagger hadn't folded—and my mind was riveted on this curious blemish and I never noticed anything about her except that. But she took my hand in hers—she was very sympathetic—and she said 'You have a great future; it will come slowly, but it will come.' And that was the last I ever saw of her. She'd said that she would re-organize her company when she came back from the tour in Europe. She'd said that she'd take me in. Only she never came back."

ANNA PAVLOVA *born January 1882 died February 1931*
"The World's Greatest Dancer"

"Every choreographer, however great, starts off with a mood of his own. And very often they use just one performer almost exclusively for a while. Fokine's muse was Karsavina. Fred, I would say, had two—the first Markova, but in a far greater way and for a much longer period, Margot Fonteyn."

NINETTE DE VALOIS

LA PÉRI

to music by Paul Dukas

During 1930 the Marie Rambert dancers appeared successfully at a variety of London theatres. Sir Nigel Playfair presented them in matinées and seasons at the Lyric Theatre, Hammersmith, and the Camargo Society's first performance depended upon the Marie Rambert dancers and the choreography of Frederick Ashton. The death of Diaghilev in the summer of 1929 had broken his company's monopoly of European ballet. Marie Rambert's company, the Camargo Society, and others benefited from the new enthusiasm with which their productions were received by audiences who could no longer depend on Diaghilev's regular visits to London.

In the spring of 1931 Marie Rambert and her playwright husband, Ashley Dukes, opened the Ballet Club in a disused church hall near Notting Hill Gate. It was, as Arnold Haskell has written, "the first permanent home of ballet in England . . . a theatre with a company and a school of its own." The Club's first, over-ambitious, season—the theatre in Ladbroke Road was still piled with builders' rubble—opened with two new works, LA PÉRI by Frederick Ashton and LE BOXING by Susan Salaman. According to contemporary accounts they were both, in different ways, successful. *The Observer's* critic described the opening as "a happy occasion" and LA PÉRI as "an engaging pseudo-Persian affair of posing peris, faint-tinkling sequins and heavenly vapours, admirably danced and excellently costumed . . . Markova danced divinely . . . and the other members of the company are as delightful as ever."

LA PÉRI, Ashton's first work for the Ballet Club, was his second new ballet for Alicia Markova and the start of their continuing working relationship. Markova had, like many other talented dancers, been left at something of a loose end by the disbanding of the Diaghilev company. She was never a member of the Marie Rambert dancers but she appeared with them as a guest artist between 1930 and 1934. Ashton was her regular partner, both in classical 'pas de deux' and in some of the ballets which he choreographed for her during this period. "She was very good to dance with," he says, "and we worked rather well together as a team. She had a wonderful technique and she was very stylish and physically we were good together because we were both rather thin and sparse." "Fred always did admire technique very much," says Marie Rambert, "and he made me bring Markova in with us and pay her a proper salary, five pounds a week. I thought it was an awful lot at the time."

Although LA PÉRI was successful at its first performances, it did not survive in its original form for long. When Markova (and later Frederick Ashton) left Rambert, the ballet was not kept in the repertoire. But in 1956 Frederick Ashton revived and re-choreographed it as a 'pas de deux' for the Royal Ballet. Margot Fonteyn danced the leading role with Michael Somes (opposite) as her partner. The photographs show this 1956 production, which also featured opulent costumes and décor by André Levasseur.

36

"The Ballet Club was really a very elegant thing. Everybody went because it was the only place with any ballet in England. We used to have the most fantastic, glittering audiences and once Fred got going at the Ballet Club, he had a very pleasant life from the point of view of not being bored. Of course, we squabbled, everybody squabbled, it was terrific, high goings-on. Small as it was, it was very lively."

WILLIAM CHAPPELL

opposite: Michael Somes, Margot Fonteyn

"Frederick Ashton started in a very small theatre and in the beginning he had to work on small, sketchy ballets without big choruses and sweeping dance steps. There wasn't room for big things and we weren't good enough. To do small, slight things when you're young and then be able to move on to serious and mature works on a larger scale is just the right way to learn. It all worked out right for him and if he had needed something different it might not have worked so well. We couldn't have danced SYMPHONIC VARIATIONS in the early 1930s. He hadn't trained us then."

MICHAEL SOMES

opposite: Michael Somes

"Our very first meeting was at a rehearsal. I remember that he came to revive LES RENDEZVOUS, which he had done about a year previously, and he started to add in a dance for four little girls. I was one of them and that was my first encounter with a choreographer at work.

"At first I thought he was absolutely mad, because he kept asking for quite impossible movements which I'd never been asked to do before. I remember running home and complaining and saying that I couldn't possibly do the things he expected.

"But no matter how impossible the things he expected, he was always able to do them himself. He was very supple and plastic in his movements and he didn't seem to have any bones at all and he would throw himself round the studio and do some twists and turns and quick little steps and then look rather exhilarated and say 'Now do what I did.' To which we'd say 'Well, what did you do?' and he'd try it again, probably rather differently."

MARGOT FONTEYN

following page: Nadia Nerina, Brian Shaw

LES RENDEZVOUS

LES RENDEZVOUS

to music by Daniel Auber

By 1931 it was already clear that Frederick Ashton was a choreographer of considerable talent and he had become a significant figure, at least on the parochial English scene. Arnold Haskell referred to him in *The Dancing Times* as "the first young choreographer of importance to have emerged since the end of the Diaghilev era", and the new ballets that Ashton created during 1930 and 1931 included FAÇADE, which proved an immediate and lasting success. After the first special performance for the Camargo Society, FAÇADE was swiftly re-produced for Marie Rambert's Ballet Club, and in 1935 Frederick Ashton's first act as resident choreographer of the Vic-Wells company was to revive this ballet. Ninette de Valois, principal choreographer, Director and Founder (with Lilian Baylis) of the Vic-Wells company from which both the Sadler's Wells company and the Royal Ballet are directly descended, had known Frederick Ashton since 1926. In the early days Ashton sometimes attended classes at de Valois' Academy of Choreographic Art and Marie Rambert remembers de Valois congratulating her, after the première of A TRAGEDY OF FASHION, on having found a "real choreographer". In 1931, although he was still principally associated with Marie Rambert and the Ballet Club, Frederick Ashton danced for de Valois in her own THE JEW IN THE BUSH and attempted his first ballet, REGATTA, for the infant Vic-Wells company. It was a success. *The Times* described it as "true-blue British romps and nautical humour".

In December, 1933, Ashton was encouraged to follow REGATTA with LES RENDEZVOUS, a more important work for which he was allotted the best cast that the Vic-Wells could provide. The ballet starred Markova, Idzikowsky, de Valois herself, and Robert Helpmann, and they were put to good use. *The Daily Telegraph*: "One could ask for nothing lighter or more delicious than the new 'divertissement', LES RENDEZVOUS, which was done for the first time last night. . . . The ballet fully deserved the ovation which it received. It gave abundant opportunity to that sort of virtuosity which can be guaranteed to bring down the house." Arnold Haskell wrote in 1937: "LES RENDEZVOUS is . . . a ballet entirely composed of arias. Its theme is brilliantly simple, meetings and partings, and admirably suited to Auber's music. It would be difficult to imagine a theme that could be more directly conveyed in movement or that could link one dance to the next in such logical and rapid succession."

Up to this time the ballets given by the Vic-Wells company had consisted principally of classical revivals and the modern ballets of Ninette de Valois. Ashton's LES RENDEZVOUS, a link between these two extremes, became a favourite. It was revived in 1937 and it is still in the repertoire of the Royal Ballet. The photographs show Nadia Nerina (opposite) and Brian Shaw in the 1959 revival.

"In my view there were three main people in that ballet world of ours —Ninette de Valois, Constant Lambert and Fred—and they worked together in a very special kind of way. She did all the administration and looked after the teaching and everything else— we don't need to talk too much about what she did, we all know— while Constant and Fred worked more closely together on the artistic and the musical side of things. It was a wonderful kind of relationship because they used to help each other, it was mutual, and it gave tremendous tone to the productions that we did. That relationship was central to Fred's work."

MICHAEL SOMES

opposite: Brian Shaw

49

LES PATINEURS

to music by Giacomo Meyerbeer, selected and arranged by Constant Lambert

In 1935 Frederick Ashton left Marie Rambert's small company to join the Vic-Wells company full time. It was a major step in his career, for Rambert's resources had always been severely limited and the Ballet Club's small stage and its tiny production budgets went hand in hand with what William Chappell remembers as "starvation wages". "Fred's mother came to me about that time," says Marie Rambert, "and said that Fred would have to go and work for a Spaniard who taught ballroom dancing, because of money. I was terribly against it. I kept saying, like Micawber, something will turn up. And something did, the best possible thing." "It was time," says Ninette de Valois, "that he had proper facilities in a professional theatre with a salary he could live on and a company that was paid to work for him. It always comes to that in the end."

Ashton's first years as the Vic-Wells company's resident choreographer were extremely successful. He no longer had to depend on working in the commercial theatre to support himself and all his energy went into a series of outstanding new ballets. LE BAISER DE LA FÉE (November, 1935) was choreographed to music by Stravinsky and featured Pearl Argyle, Harold Turner and a relative newcomer called Margot Fonteyn. APPARITIONS (February, 1936) established Robert Helpmann and Margot Fonteyn as a partnership of extraordinary promise and introduced Cecil Beaton to the problems of designing for a full-sized theatre. NOCTURNE (November, 1936) was, like LE BAISER DE LA FÉE, designed by Sophie Fedorovitch. It is remembered as one of her most successful settings, but it was also at this time that Ashton's working relationship with Margot Fonteyn matured and began successfully to develop. Frederick Ashton has said that in his early contacts with Fonteyn he found her "stubborn, elegant, unyielding, lacking in sharpness—but musical". His doubts about her ability to replace Alicia Markova, who had left the Vic-Wells in 1935, began to evaporate after her success in NOCTURNE. She was still only sixteen years old. Frederick Ashton's next major ballet for the Vic-Wells company was LES PATINEURS, less ambitious but longer-lasting than the three mentioned above. This witty sketch in ballet of the activities on a frozen pond received a rapturous reception when it was presented in February, 1937. Curiously enough, Ashton claimed never to have visited a skating rink when he created this work. If so it did not stop him creating a style of movement which authentically suggests the accidents and acrobatics of skaters of both sexes and all types. The principal role, originally danced by Harold Turner, is one of the most flamboyant parts for a male dancer which Ashton has created, but the ballet is not a star vehicle in any way. Instead, as Mary Clarke has written: "It is a lasting tribute to the high level the company had reached by the beginning of 1937."

LES PATINEURS has always been popular and it is still in the repertoire of the Royal Ballet. The photographs show the former 'touring section' of the Royal Ballet at a performance in January, 1970. Alan Hooper was the Blue Skater (Harold Turner's original part) while Shirley Grahame and Barry McGrath appeared in roles created by Margot Fonteyn and Robert Helpmann. The costumes and décor are as originally designed in the 1930s by William Chappell.

above: Barry McGrath, Shirley Grahame

above: Alan Hooper
opposite: Katheryn Wade, Sally Inkin

CONSTANT LAMBERT *born August 1905 died August 1951*

"My personal opinion is that Constant Lambert's name has not been given nearly enough importance in the history of the growth and success of the British ballet. Since I've become a Director of the Australian ballet I realize how lucky we were to have him in the early days at the Vic-Wells. He influenced everybody's musical taste and he was also a great conductor of ballet music and raised the standards of accompaniment at the theatre out of all recognition. He loved the ballet and he devoted his life to it and because of this he doesn't have the reputation as a serious musician that he should have.

"Musically there wasn't a question that you could ask Constant Lambert that he couldn't answer. He knew an enormous amount and he was very decisive indeed about music. He would lay down the law to all of us and there were certain things he would conduct and other things he wouldn't touch. He kept us on the rails and almost all Fred's early ballets show Constant's influence."

ROBERT HELPMANN

"When I first met Constant Lambert he'd already done a ballet for Diaghilev and one for Nijinska. He was a great figure to me and I was thrilled to work with him and very happy with POMONA, which we did for the Camargo Society, because it saved the evening.

"At that time Constant was very beautiful, or at least I thought so. He had this marvellous head and he always wore bright shirts like people do today, which was revolutionary. He made an enormous impact on me as a human being because he had an extraordinary sense of humour and he was always very positive in his opinions, especially if music was involved. He had a tremendous potency about him and he was the most intellectual person I'd ever met. He was a friend of the Sitwells and all the Bloomsbury set and he was knowledgeable in all branches of art and literature. He was somebody you could feed off. Lord Keynes once told me that he considered Constant the most potentially brilliant man he'd ever met, and I'm sure he was right.

"Constant Lambert really loved the ballet. Most musicians at that time thought it was slightly *infra dig.* to conduct for ballet but when I went to the Wells I practically saw Constant daily. He contributed enormously. With APPARITIONS we worked on the score together, because it was Liszt, which we were both keen on. With LES RENDEZVOUS I rather think that I suggested Auber but he did the final selection. And then with PATINEURS he was going to give that score to Ninette because I was supposed to tackle THE RAKE'S PROGRESS. Only I heard him playing PATINEURS after a matinée and I kept saying 'That's not for her. that's not for her.' Eventually Ninette and I managed a swop, which was better for both of us."

FREDERICK ASHTON

"It was very exciting to be present at rehearsals in the thirties. The whole thing was great fun— Fred wasn't worried and I wasn't worried and everything was in full spate. I think it was a very productive period, full of activity and excitement and influences of all kinds."

CECIL BEATON

56

"In the old days, before the war, he was always describing how Pavlova or Karsavina or Spessit-seva had done a step or a movement and he was always trying to impersonate and show and saying 'Why can't you do it like this?' He was always inspiring one and goading one to do things and a great deal of what we learned when we were young came from Fred's descriptions and impersonations of dancers he had seen."

MARGOT FONTEYN

"We still get what he saw of Pavlova in years past thrown at our heads. He's still apt to get up and run across the room and say 'Oh, none of you can run like Pavlova.'"

"Fred is absolutely marvellous at conjuring up the way certain people of different epochs behave. He is a born choreographer in that some people use words but he, rather than describe something, will mime it. And very often he will mime the most banal and ordinary everyday events but by his insistence and by the authority with which he does this very simple thing he completely disarms you. His timing and the fact that he is so assured beat down your resistance and you just give in and roar with laughter. One laughs an awful lot in his company."

CECIL BEATON

"Fred is enormously observant. With a choreographer it's all a question of the eye and he uses his all the time. He stores up impressions and all sorts of ideas for when he needs them and as a result he has a tremendous sense of style and a very visual memory. When he suggests something he often says 'I saw my mother do it like that' or 'I used to see people walking in the Park like that.' Even now he'll go and watch people and pick up what they do and embellish it and he's very clever in making use of all the sources of inspiration which there are. He always listens to casual conversation in the Tube and he puts all that into his ballets."

MICHAEL SOMES

A WEDDING BOUQUET

to words by Gertrude Stein and music by Lord Berners

In 1934, Frederick Ashton worked outside Britain for the first time. "Through some American friends I met the composer Virgil Thomson in London when he was working on FOUR SAINTS IN THREE ACTS with Gertrude Stein. I suggested things to him and five months later he cabled me to come over. I wasn't busy and I wanted to go to New York, which was a wonderful, invigorating place in those days, and I accepted. It was a terrible task—the most exhausting job I ever did. But it was a great success."

Three years later, back in England, Ashton created a ballet which used Gertrude Stein's THEY MUST BE WEDDED TO THEIR WIFE as its libretto. "WEDDING BOUQUET really had no connection at all with FOUR SAINTS. Gerald Berners had met Gertrude Stein and, like all of us, he was fascinated by her and he had this idea for a ballet. It was only afterwards that I came into it."

Lord Berners, one of the talented and unusual people whom Ashton had met through Constant Lambert, made a very special contribution to A WEDDING BOUQUET. He designed the costumes and wrote the music and it was Lord Berners who encouraged Ashton to use Gertrude Stein's fragmented, funny and occasionally relevant account of a French provincial wedding as a counterpoint to the action of the ballet. *The Times* wrote, after the ballet's 1937 première: "Everyone laughed at this (the commentary) as they laughed at everything else in the burlesque. The costumes, designed by Lord Berners, are caricatures as extraordinary as his parodies of waltz and tango." However great Lord Berners' initial contribution, it was Ashton's sharp and witty choreography which welded the diverse elements of A WEDDING BOUQUET into a whole. Ashton had lived and worked in France and, through his mother's family, had French connections. Each of the guests at the wedding is an exuberant, light-hearted and detailed caricature and their celebration is extravagantly depicted. *The Daily Telegraph*: "Ashton's choreography is ingenious and something more. He has given a sharp point to the librettist's sources; but he has not relied on the fun alone, or gone in for the grotesque, as a lesser artist would have been tempted to do. His movement is always harmonious and often beautiful, the humour is provided by some delicate touches of mime, and the lifts, in particular, are very original. The ballet does not set itself up to be a great and enduring work . . . but it could be called a great collaboration."

The original cast of A WEDDING BOUQUET was one of the largest which Ashton had used in his own works, and it reads now like the roll of honour of British ballet. Principal dancers included Margot Fonteyn as Julia, Robert Helpmann as the Bridegroom, June Brae as the drunken Josephine, Ninette de Valois as Webster, and Harold Turner, Pamela May, William Chappell, Michael Somes and Leslie Edwards as guests, friends, or relatives.

The photographs were taken during the 1969 revival of A WEDDING BOUQUET. Robert Helpmann, following in Constant Lambert's footsteps, spoke the narrative through a microphone, while Ann Jenner was Julia, and Jennifer Penney and Alexander Grant played the Bride and Bridegroom (opposite); Deanne Bergsma was Josephine and Monica Mason Webster; Leslie Edwards was also in the cast.

"Fred's ballets are real dancing. He never seems to lose his gift for movement and he's always surprising you and doing something different."

WILLIAM CHAPPELL

"In the early days, and I'm only talking about the early days, he was inclined to wander away from the story in favour of the movement. Of all the elements in a ballet it was the story line he was inclined to gloss over."

ROBERT HELPMANN

above: Robert Helpmann
opposite: Alexander Grant, Jennifer Penney

"I think that Fred's main weakness in the very early days was a certain lack of follow-through. You'd find yourself saying 'But you can't finish it like that' and he was quite capable of replying 'Well, I'm tired of it anyway.' He had a tendency to lose his scenario half-way through and I don't mind anyone changing the story, but if you lose it you've got to replace it."

NINETTE DE VALOIS

"He's very self-conscious now about telling a story and he tries quite hard to get the feel of it across. But style and atmosphere are more important to him than narrative. These are the things he does best. He can tell a good story but ballet's never very good at telling stories, is it? It's an art of atmosphere and style."

MICHAEL SOMES

opposite: Ann Jenner

"Of course nowadays standards are high. But in the early days everybody was very individual. Everybody had style. We were all good performers and Fred had learned to make the most of what we could offer."

WILLIAM CHAPPELL

opposite: Alexander Grant, Jennifer Penney
below: Deanne Bergsma

"In 1933, when I first met Fred, British ballet hadn't started to become smart. Normally we only did one performance a week, and we were forced to work in the commercial theatre for the rest of the time. We all did revues as often as we could get them. Company salaries were non-existent and we just had to lead a much less sheltered life than dancers do today. We knew about the theatre in all its forms. I remember seeing Fred in one of Cochran's midnight shows at the Trocadero, and very good he was, too. People say that I have a marvellous sense of the theatre. A great deal of it I learned from Fred."

ROBERT HELPMANN

above: David Drew, Kenneth Mason, Monica Mason
opposite: Deanne Bergsma
following page: Ann Jenner, Alexander Grant, Jennifer Penney

"Things were very different before the war. Ninette, I believe, would come along and say 'Now, Fred, I want a romantic ballet at Christmas and then a twenty-minute abstract ballet by Easter.' And he went away and did it. Nowadays they don't do that. You have to go round and say 'Well, dear, do you think you'd like to do a ballet? Would you go away and think what you'd like to do?' In those days you worked to order, which was marvellous, and as a result he doesn't ever have to wait for God to speak or any of that sort of thing or inspiration to drop. He's very practical and professional and if you say 'Now look, you've got to do this bit today,' he'll do it then."

MICHAEL SOMES

"He had a great advantage over the young choreo-graphers of today—he really had. There was no repertoire —there was a vacuum and we practically produced ballets alternately at one time. The work had to be done, whereas now it's almost impossible to find a place to work in. That was his great advantage and Fred always had the application to make the most of it. I don't know a harder worker and I don't know anyone who is less interested in money or comfort. He was marvellous, just like every-body at the Wells. There would never have been a Royal Ballet if we hadn't been like that."

NINETTE DE VALOIS

FREDERICK ASHTON IN CONVERSATION

THE THIRTIES AND THE WAR

"I must say, the death of Diaghilev was an enormous shock. I was in the South of France when I heard, and I was horrified. But in a strange way it was the best thing that could have happened. I don't think the English revival would ever have taken place if he had lived. It wasn't that there was any immediate surge of interest in English ballet, but the things we were starting had a chance of attracting some sort of audience and what did happen very strikingly was that Diaghilev's dancers appeared in England. That was how I came to work with Karsavina and Markova and Lopokova and Dolin. Otherwise I would never have got the chance.

"I got a tremendous amount out of all that in the early thirties, especially when I worked with Karsavina. Her whole approach and her marvellous acting ability and everything about her impressed me enormously. I used to watch her from the wings in everything she did. Her grandeur! She rehearsed me in CARNAVAL and in LES SYLPHIDES, which I danced with her, and I got a great feeling for the fluidity and continuity of movement in LES SYLPHIDES which Fokine wanted. But I was tremendously in awe when I came to work with her. My first ballet for her was MERCURY, at the Lyric, Hammersmith in 1930, and I really found it very frightening to tackle such a great dancer who had worked with Fokine and Massine and everybody else. I was rather too aware of her glorious past to be comfortable. It was like being asked to do a ballet on the Queen.

"In Rambert's little group and at the Ballet Club I remember that we were all terribly young and frivolous and enthusiastic and we used to laugh and joke a great deal. Of course, somebody was always in tears and I was always having rows, but it was quite a happy period. I started to get a pittance for doing Camargo Society ballets and Nigel Playfair put us on every so often. I suppose I danced about once a month at that time and everything was makeshift and improvised. The costumes for A FLORENTINE PICTURE were made of old curtains and the material for the costumes for CAPRIOL SUITE came from Pontings' or Barkers' sale. In LA PÉRI the coat I wore had belonged to Princess Galitzin. It was an evening coat in marvellous brocade which she gave us because she was a friend of Marie Rambert.

"The trouble was that I was a little against the Ballet Club when it started. I begged Rambert to be more active in the professional theatre because I found the club constricting and I longed to get away. I wanted a wider field and a bigger stage. That was where Ninette was sensible. She got a proper theatre, instead of occasional performances with a piano. One wanted more than that.

"It was totally different from the Ballet Club at the Wells. Lopokova used to call Ninette's little troupe 'the ugly ducklings'. They were all efficient, while Rambert's girls were beautiful. However, the Wells was generally an improvement. It gave me security. It gave me a regular salary, which I hadn't had before, and I was immensely appreciative of the luxury of using proper dancers at last and having proper facilities. It was very stimulating working with Constant and Sophie Fedorovitch and having de Valois there and the whole thing growing and expanding and getting better.

"It was also when I got to the Wells, about this time, that my mother started, not to be encouraging exactly, but to come to all the performances and to be critical of my work. When I'd finished something she'd say 'I don't understand. What was that supposed to mean?' She wanted everything explained, which used to irritate me terribly. But sometimes she was right—it needed explaining. She was highly intelligent and she could see just what was happening and she was also very musical—she played the piano very well.

"It was the first time that she had really come to be in sympathy with what I was doing. She had been discouraging for a long time, because we had no money and nowhere to live. I'd had to fight that. I always felt a little resentful about my brothers because of that—they hadn't helped me with her at all—and eventually I rather cut myself off from them. They always say how cold I am. But it goes back to that pre-war period, when things were really very hard.

"My mother died in 1939, just before the war. So I was independent at last, although it didn't do me any good. Almost as soon as the war started I had to go into the R.A.F. Everyone was being called up—all the dancers and everyone I knew in the theatre—and I wanted, I suppose, to share their agony. I must say, I thought it was the end of everything. It was a period of enormous frustration to me because I felt I hadn't said nearly enough to be ready to die on it.

"The importance of the war was that it gave me a period to think and read a good deal and also, because I was rather unhappy, I went in for mysticism. I read St Theresa of Avila and St John of the Cross and lots of books about mystics and mysticism. After all, one was told that it was the end of the world.

"During the war, the tendency in all the ballets seemed to become much too literary and dramatic. During the last part of the war I was stationed at the Air Ministry as an Intelligence officer and I saw everything that was going on, although at this stage I couldn't do any work myself. It was very frustrating, and originally I think that SYMPHONIC VARIATIONS was very much over-choreographed. I remember doing a tremendous amount of eliminating, especially in the finale; I pared and pared and pared until I got the kind of purity I wanted. You see, when I started I was going to do something very complicated, with lots of people and a sort of seasonal theme. But then I thought one day that six dancers would be enough. When one begins to do things one is apt to overcharge everything, and if things are too intense, one blurs the vision of the audience. By simplifying, you make it easier for an audience to take in your intentions.

"With SYMPHONIC VARIATIONS I had to do a lot of experimenting to find the sort of movement that I wanted. That was what took the time, but once I had achieved it the rest went fairly well. I was able to ride on the music quite a bit because I knew it very well and I'd listened to it during the war. I'd always hoped I would get round to using it one day."

SYMPHONIC VARIATIONS

to music by César Franck

SYMPHONIC VARIATIONS, one of Frederick Ashton's most important ballets, was first performed in April, 1946, at the new post-war home of the Sadler's Wells Ballet—the Royal Opera House, Covent Garden. A contemporary review refers to its first night as "the choreographic event not only of this but of many years", and SYMPHONIC VARIATIONS is the work by which Ashton regained and re-created his pre-war reputation.

Before the war some critics were inclined to dismiss Frederick Ashton as a lightweight. Arnold Haskell, writing in 1937, compared Ashton unfavourably with Ninette de Valois: "She had a great deal to express and found difficulty in doing so," he wrote, "he had very little to say but did so with extraordinary charm." C. W. Beaumont, writing about a pre-war ballet, accused Ashton of "an insatiable desire to be amusing in the fashionable sense of the word".

Frederick Ashton, faced with these comments and with Mary Clarke's description of his Ballet Club output as "beautiful, charming, elegant, rather heartless works", replies: "I wouldn't accept 'heartless' for one moment, but I won't deny that a lot of my pre-war ballets were very light. I had a terror of boring people and I wasn't concerned with being profound. The twenties and thirties were a very frivolous period and I wasn't trying to correct this—I just went with it."

After the war circumstances, and perhaps Ashton, changed. "When the war ended," says William Chappell, "I found that Fred was a much quieter and graver man. He didn't lose his sense of humour and he's still marvellously good fun, but it did show at the time." Margot Fonteyn does not remember that Ashton changed. "Fred is a real artist," she says, "in that he absorbs everything around him and it comes out in his work. Before the war, things were very carefree. After the war, economics started to come into it much more. The company was on its way to becoming a major international ballet company. I would say that everything changed, rather than that Fred changed."

Whatever Ashton's personal development, SYMPHONIC VARIATIONS was a landmark in his career. His gift for bold, intense and sustained choreographic invention has never been put to better use than in this outwardly simple, abstract work which Sophie Fedorovitch dressed and decorated so aptly. He has described it as "a sort of testament", and it is a ballet in which the dancing reigns supreme and the seminal theme always remained, in Clive Barnes' words, at the back of Ashton's notebook. SYMPHONIC VARIATIONS is the work by which Ashton re-stated and refreshed his own classicism and welded it into his strongest weapon, capable, in its own terms, of dealing even with the turmoil of the war. In the years that have followed, every ballet that he has made has communicated his faith in classical dancing to audience and performers. Perhaps, fancifully, one can compare Ashton's intentions in SYMPHONIC VARIATIONS with Diaghilev's intentions when he revived THE SLEEPING BEAUTY after the First World War.

If only one Ashton ballet could be preserved, SYMPHONIC VARIATIONS might represent his work at its very best. But Margot Fonteyn (opposite) would, ideally, always be in the cast. In the original production she was joined by Pamela May and Moira Shearer and their partners were Michael Somes, Henry Danton and Brian Shaw.

"When SYMPHONIC VARIATIONS was almost finished, Michael Somes had to have an operation on the cartilage in his knee. The first night of SYMPHONIC was postponed for something like two months while Michael had his operation and got back into training.

"When we started to rehearse it all again Fred took out a lot of things and simplified and purified the choreography. Instead of having his usual deadline for the dress rehearsal and the first performance he had time to re-assess the choreography. I think that's one reason why it turned out to be one of his masterpieces. I remember a lot of discussion and all sorts of different ideas and versions and several different endings and Sophie Fedorovitch at the rehearsals and coming in each day to say what she thought. A lot went into revising SYMPHONIC. It's probably the only ballet he's ever had the opportunity to revise before the first night."

MARGOT FONTEYN

previous page: Antoinette Sibley, Annette Page, Georgina Parkinson
opposite: Michael Somes, Anya Linden, Margot Fonteyn
following page: David Blair, Margot Fonteyn

"It's very hard to get choreographers to revise their ballets after they've done them. With SYMPHONIC Fred got down to all sorts of things while he was waiting, working by a process of elimination, as all great choreographers seem to. Their canvas is overcrowded with too much material and too many ideas and then they simplify it."

NINETTE DE VALOIS

above: Donald MacLeary, Antoinette Sibley
opposite: Donald MacLeary

86

"With a choreographer like Fred it's a matter of taste whether you like his comic ballets or his classical ballets or his other ballets best. I suppose most people think that SYMPHONIC VARIATIONS is his masterpiece. Very likely it is, but how can you compare it? It's totally different from some other things he's done and some of his works were very great at a particular time. I think that DANTE SONATA was a marvellous ballet when it was done, in 1940, but it was revived after the war with dancers who didn't live through that period and they really didn't know what it was about. It wouldn't keep."

MARGOT FONTEYN

"The great thing about Fred is that he is very versatile, yet this has never stopped him being a master in all the styles he uses. In all the fields of ballet, dramatic, comic, classical, abstract, you can find at least one of his works which is truly masterly. Very few other choreographers have been able to cover such a wide range so successfully."
MICHAEL SOMES

CINDERELLA

to music by Serge Prokofiev

Frederick Ashton's ballets do not always seem to respond to the demands of the critics, and at certain periods of his career he has suffered severely at the hands of the press. Before the war his wit and his emphasis on 'pure dancing' were interpreted as shallowness. After the war, his early promise was immediately fulfilled in SYMPHONIC VARIATIONS. But almost everything he attempted after that was compared unfavourably, at least by implication, with that unique ballet.
LES SIRÈNES, which Ashton created in November, 1946, was, like A WEDDING BOUQUET, to music by Lord Berners. But the fun in LES SIRÈNES quite swamped the ballet. "It was a flop," says Cecil Beaton, its designer, "the trouble was that it was badly timed. If it had been given six years later, people would have enjoyed it but at that time they were in a serious mood. They couldn't accept it as just a 'blague'— they missed the joke and thought it was a waste of all our talents."
SCÈNES DE BALLET, presented in February, 1948, also received a cool critical reception which it has successfully outlived. But LES SIRÈNES foundered altogether after its reviews and DON JUAN, premièred in November, 1948, was not a success either. Mary Clarke has described it as "superficially elegant ... with no real heart or drive to it". In this unpromising atmosphere, Ashton, encouraged by de Valois, initiated his most ambitious project. CINDERELLA, which was premièred in December, 1948, was the first three-act ballet which an English choreographer had made. By attempting it Ashton risked direct comparison with the classical ballets of Petipa and Ivanov and challenged the twentieth century convention that only one-act ballets could be artistically and commercially profitable. It was, reassuringly, an enormous success. One of Frederick Ashton's strengths is his ability to bring fresh material within the scope of classical ballet. The well-known story of CINDERELLA, the central comic duo—straight from the pantomime—and the touching leading role for the ballerina have made the work acceptable and welcome to several generations of ballet audiences. When CINDERELLA was premièred *The Daily Telegraph*'s critic wrote, without apparent irony, "There is understandably less here for the adult mind than in Ashton's other works." But CINDERELLA has always been more than a Christmas frolic for children and adolescents. "A brilliant addition to the mounting tale of English ballets," wrote *The Times* in 1948. Moira Shearer, who took over after Margot Fonteyn was injured, played the leading role in CINDERELLA at the première. With her were Pamela May, as the Fairy Godmother, and Nadia Nerina, Violetta Elvin, Pauline Clayden and Beryl Grey as the Fairy Seasons. Michael Somes played the Prince and Alexander Grant the Jester. Robert Helpmann and Frederick Ashton danced as the Ugly Sisters. The photographs show three different ballerinas in the leading role of CINDERELLA, Margot Fonteyn (opposite), Svetlana Beriosova, and Antoinette Sibley who, with Anthony Dowell as her Prince, danced at the 1969 revival. Georgina Parkinson appears as the Fairy Godmother and Robert Helpmann and Frederick Ashton play the Ugly Sisters.

"It must be a great relief for an audience to see different ballets coming out of the same choreographer. It doesn't make much difference to the dancers but I think it's a great relief for the audience."
MARGOT FONTEYN

Frederick Ashton, Leslie Edwards, Robert Helpmann

"The big hit of Ashton's CINDERELLA is his pair of Ugly Sisters, Ashton and Helpmann, and it is the one whom Ashton plays . . . who becomes the charmer of the evening. She is the shyest, the happiest, most innocent of monsters. She adores the importance of scolding, the fluster of getting dressed up in a rush of milliners, hairdressers, jewellers; to do a little dance step transports her, though she keeps forgetting what comes next. Such a monster wins everybody's heart. Ashton does it reticently, with perfect timing and the apparently tentative gesture, the absorption and sweetness of nature of the great clown. It is as if he never meant to be the star of the show, and very likely he didn't. He cast Helpmann, England's greatest mime, as the first step-sister. He gave that part the initiative in their scenes. He himself was only to trail along vaguely, with one solo in the second act. After all, he was busy at the time choreographing the three acts of his, and England's, first full length classical ballet, and doing it in six weeks. Ashton's unexpected triumph on the stage is the sort of accident that happens to geniuses."

EDWIN DENBY—*BALLET* February 1949

-"Frederick Ashton has always choreographed more on his artists than on paper. Consequently there is a great sense of harmony and beauty in his compositions. Naturally, since he's a very sensitive person and doesn't preconceive his ballets he's influenced by his material and by the character of his dancers. But this aspect has been exaggerated. Too many of his ballets have survived too many first-class casts for one to accept that he was specially dependent on his original artists."

NINETTE DE VALOIS

above: Georgina Parkinson
opposite: Svetlana Beriosova

"As far as I'm concerned, Fred is perfect to work with. He allows you to do your own characterization and then he moulds it. He doesn't attempt to *impose* anything. Choreographically, he insists, quite naturally, on his line and his method of doing things. But some choreographers superimpose the characterization on you and you simply feel you're in a cage. You feel that anybody could do it. When Fred creates a part you feel he does it for you. And sometimes, in certain ballets, it can work badly. Because if somebody has contributed outstandingly in one of his ballets, the ballet loses something if they go."

ROBERT HELPMANN

below: Svetlana Beriosova
opposite: Anthony Dowell, Antoinette Sibley
following page: Antoinette Sibley

"Fred uses every artist in the best possible way—the best that he or she can offer—and we know him so well that we can also give him a little bit during the process." SVETLANA BERIOSOVA

"More often than not, the cast list of a new ballet is only put up when the ballet has been finished. You hear that there's a new ballet coming up but you don't know whether you're in it until you're called to a rehearsal; by that time the choreographer might be half-way through and, particularly with Sir Frederick's ballets, I come into the rehearsal room and very little is said. He doesn't explain the part or the ballet or anything. You just get a feeling for it from the first thing he tells you to do. You get an idea of what he wants and you know that you can try this or that or anything and if it is wrong or it isn't what he wants, he will tell you. You see, he has the most marvellous eye. And you know this and you know that you can trust his eye. As a result, you feel very free. You can attempt anything, no matter how awful, because he won't let you do it if it isn't right. That's the secret. That's why he can get us to do things we wouldn't try for another choreographer. In the end he always shows us off to advantage and so we attempt things that wouldn't normally be within our scope."

ALEXANDER GRANT

below: Frederick Ashton, Robert Helpmann
opposite: Donald MacLeary, Svetlana Beriosova, Georgina Parkinson
following page: Antoinette Sibley, Anthony Dowell

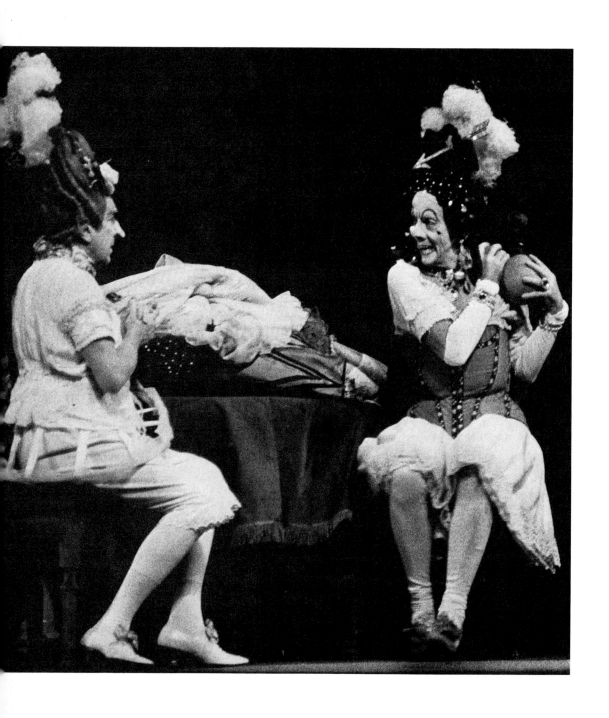

"Of course, Fred was never a ballet master. He had the knowledge, but he wasn't that sort of person. What he could do was show you how to use whatever minimal technique you had to advantage. However tiny your talent, he found something you could do that would look good. And as the Company has changed and new dancers have emerged, he has always been not only equal to these demands, but well ahead. The dancers have always had to come up to his standards, but even when they have he's still been looking forward. He has never said 'Oh, there's a marvellous dancer, now what is there for that dancer to do?' He'd always been there before us."

MICHAEL SOMES

ANTHONY DOWELL

in

DAPHNIS AND CHLOË

"The dramatic element in Ashton is but of small importance to the whole. Strip his ballets of their programmes, perform them in practice dress in front of dull curtains and the pattern of his choreography would still convey its emotion, still possess its beauty."

CLIVE BARNES
(from 'Ballet in Britain since the War')

109

DAPHNIS AND CHLOË

to music by Maurice Ravel

In October, 1949, the Sadler's Wells Ballet began its first, revelatory tour of North America with a performance of THE SLEEPING BEAUTY in New York. Ashton danced as Carabosse at the first night and he received the most expansive reception of his twin careers as choreographer and dancer during this outrageously successful season and tour. FAÇADE was a particular success with the American public and so was ILLUMINATIONS, to which he turned immediately the tour was over.

ILLUMINATIONS, based on poems by Arthur Rimbaud and music by Benjamin Britten, was the first ballet that he created for the New York City Ballet, the company of George Balanchine and Lincoln Kirstein. The Sadler's Wells tours of America and Ashton's work for the New York City Ballet set the seal on his international reputation as a choreographer. In the 1950 Birthday Honours he was named Commander of the Order of the British Empire, the first man to receive this honour for services to ballet.

Recently, writing in the *New York Times*, Clive Barnes has suggested that the Royal Ballet has two real homes. In New York, he says, the company is as lively and alert as a philanderer's mistress. In London, on the other hand, it behaves, and to some extent is treated, like a neglected wife. After the flattering attentions of the Americans, Ashton's first three new ballets back in England made little impression on the London audiences and critics. DAPHNIS AND CHLOË was followed during 1951 by TIRESIAS, his final collaboration with Constant Lambert, and by a sumptuous revision and revival of CASSE NOISETTE. DAPHNIS AND CHLOË was especially unjustly dismissed when it was premièred. It had little success until its New York première in 1953.

There were perhaps two reasons for Ashton's initial interest in DAPHNIS AND CHLOË. The first, and most important, was the music. Ravel's score is one of the few undoubted masterpieces composed specifically for ballet but by the time it was completed in 1912, Diaghilev, who had commissioned it, was passionately involved with Nijinsky's first steps in choreography. He was much less interested in Fokine's plans and Fokine's production of DAPHNIS AND CHLOË had no particular success, Frederick Ashton never saw it and made no attempt to re-create it and Ravel's glorious music was the only lasting legacy of Fokine's project. "Here was a great score," says Frederick Ashton, "that was what really decided me on it. I thought that its proper place was in the theatre and not the concert hall."

DAPHNIS AND CHLOË, like many of Ashton's ballets, is built around the ballerina's role. Perhaps this was the second reason for Ashton's interest. Margot Fonteyn had had an enormous success during the Sadler's Wells Ballet's first tours of North America. But she excelled herself as Chloë and Frederick Ashton excelled his previous creations for her. Strangely enough, even this great ballerina role was not admired in 1951.

The original cast of DAPHNIS AND CHLOË included Michael Somes as Daphnis, John Field as the aggressive Dorkon and Violetta Elvin as Lykanion the seductress. Alexander Grant played Bryaxis, the brigand chief. In the photographs, taken during the most recent revival, Anthony Dowell and Antoinette Sibley (opposite) play the leading roles. Merle Park also appears as Chloë. Alexander Grant plays his original role, as he has in every revival of the ballet since 1951.

"The first new production that I took part in was when Sir Frederick was doing DAPHNIS AND CHLOË. I was made understudy to a shepherd boy who happened to hurt his back on the day before the dress rehearsal. I found I had to do the dress rehearsal and I remember that I was at the Opera House very early; I met Sir Frederick and he said 'Do you know the role well enough?' I said 'I think so.' He didn't say anything more, but after the dress rehearsal he came round and thanked me. It was the first time he'd addressed me personally. If I was ever noticed as a dancer that's how it all began."

DESMOND DOYLE

opposite: Anthony Dowell, Antoinette Sibley

"I suppose the only point of friction between Fred and me was the second cast. It's the history of all directors and choreographers in any company. The choreographer would always prefer the first cast and it's only choreographers who've also directed who bring on the second cast automatically. The choreographer sees it like painting a picture. There it is, complete with the original cast, and he doesn't want any changes. When Fred was young he always thought we shouldn't perform the ballet if they all went down with flu. But you just can't run a theatre like that. It's worse than in a play because accidents are much more numerous—you could twist your ankle or sprain your wrist and act, but any stupid little accident stops you dancing. Even Fred realized that in time. He'd originally been used to working in the Ballet Club, where it was personal. Once he got into a bigger theatre he began to realize that the show had to go on."

NINETTE DE VALOIS

above: Anthony Dowell
opposite: Antoinette Sibley

"As Director, Ninette was always worried when Fred did a new ballet. Dancers are always subject to injury and Ninette wanted someone to learn the new roles as they were done. She was always trying to put on the second cast and Fred was always doing his best to stop her. He wanted his first cast that had created the ballet because he had this genius for casting a ballet really well, picking the right people within the company and then bringing out their best points to complement the ballet and the characters he was sketching. Ninette used to annoy Sir Frederick a terrific amount, because she insisted."

ALEXANDER GRANT

above: Marguerite Porter, Vergie Derman, Ria Peri
opposite: Merle Park
following page: Alexander Grant

"I've never known a great choreographer not start his career wanting to be a dancer. I don't think anyone really starts off to be a choreographer. You dance and then you suddenly find that you have an interest in movement for movement's sake. You find yourself doing ballets in which you find that something's awkward and think you'd like to change it. And then of course you suddenly find a great interest in music and you find yourself listening to music and automatically choreographing to it in your head. I suppose everyone starts like that. And Fred's interest in dancing was very strong. I think he was pushed into being a choreographer at the beginning. He didn't rush at it, but it's not always the very talented people that rush at it—just the opposite!"

NINETTE DE VALOIS

opposite: David Drew, Antoinette Sibley, Anthony Dowell

"If you had any question of what was right and what was wrong Sophie Fedorovitch was the person you asked, not only about the theatre but about life. She was a mysterious, extraordinary influence on everybody she came in touch with."

ROBERT HELPMANN

SOPHIE FEDOROVITCH *born 1893 died January 1953*

"By her death I lost not only my dearest friend but my greatest artistic collaborator and adviser. She was the ideal ballet designer. . . ."

FREDERICK ASHTON
(from 'Sophie Fedorovitch' by Simon Fleet)

"I think that Sophie Fedorovitch was an enormous help to Fred, a real support. At rehearsal he relied very much on her judgment because she was very careful and very intelligent and she had very good taste. She always considered everything carefully and weighed everything up and whereas Fred was involved with the movement Sophie *thought* about everything. Fred had to have the dancers there and move them and see the effect but Sophie would ponder on things and weigh up which moment was right or which moment needed some amplification or which could be simplified. She was perhaps better able to do that than Fred and so she was able to supplement Fred's own feelings and judgment. In her own work, of course, she was another person. She simplified and refined everything she did and she would think for days sometimes about adding a little piece of grey net down one side of a costume or putting a very fragile coloured bow on one shoulder."

MARGOT FONTEYN

"No matter how modern his ballets are, his line is basically classical. His love of the classical dance is paramount, and this goes back to Pavlova. Every ballet that Fred choreographed, one knew or one saw that the principal female role would have been ideal for Pavlova. Next time you talk to him, ask him about it. Because I did and he said 'Yes, of course she would have been wonderful. Because I think of her when I'm working all the time.'"

ROBERT HELPMANN

below: Margot Fonteyn and Frederick Ashton—a curtain call at the Maryinsky Theatre, Leningrad, after the Russian première of ONDINE on 15 June, 1961.

ONDINE

to music by Hans Werner Henze

Frederick Ashton's final apprenticeship as a choreographer was served during the late 1940s. Clive Barnes has singled out the plotless ballets, SYMPHONIC VARIATIONS, SCÉNES DE BALLET and VALSES NOBLES ET SENTIMENTALES, as marking an important stage in his development, and the first full-length ballets are also landmarks. CINDERELLA (1948) was followed by SYLVIA (1952) and ROMEO AND JULIET (1955), for the Royal Danish Ballet.

But during the 1950s Ashton's progress was, to a certain extent, interrupted. In 1953, on one of his rare ventures into production, he worked with Kathleen Ferrier on Gluck's opera ORPHEUS. It was her last appearance. Sophie Fedorovitch also died at this period, and Constant Lambert had died two years previously, at the age of forty-six. These were heavy blows, and Michael Somes has identified this period as a crucial watershed. "I think then he realized that he was getting to be more on his own—and that is a very difficult moment of truth for a lot of artists. . . . After Sophie and Constant died he turned very much to Margot Fonteyn and to his dancers, to the people under him."

Frederick Ashton and Margot Fonteyn had been close friends, as well as colleagues, since the late 1930s. She talks about him with enormous insight and she sees him as someone eternally beset by a subdued sense of life's ironies and disappointments. "I think Fred's perfect day would always contain a few moments of melancholia and regret because it hadn't been quite perfect."

During the 1940s and 1950s, Ashton's close relationship with Margot Fonteyn was a unique influence on his creative output. CINDERELLA, DAPHNIS AND CHLOË and many of his other major ballets were sharply focussed on her talents. ONDINE, Ashton's fourth full-length ballet, premièred in October, 1958, was the climax of their work together. She has said that Ondine was the most sympathetic of all the characters that Frederick Ashton created for her, and her role, as a water nymph whose liaison with a mortal ends in disaster, stood out from and, in a sense, exposed the other elements of the ballet.

One feature of the Maryinsky tradition which Anna Pavlova emphasized was the importance of the ballerina. As Pavlova, by force of circumstance and inclination, made ballets revolve round her, so Ashton seems to have designed ONDINE as a foil for Fonteyn. Her dancing had both to sustain and revitalize the early nineteenth-century fairy tale on which the work was based and she was surrounded by shadowy, almost undrawn, characters while she attempted this. Not all critics found that even Fonteyn could accomplish such a task. Ninette de Valois describes ONDINE as "outstanding, with reservations. It's got a wonderful theme of water carried through from beginning to end and for me it has an almost mystical quality about it, such difficult music too, so beautifully rendered. Of course, it does drop choreographically in places, but there are some beautiful passages of ensemble work as well as a role for Fonteyn which could never be equalled."

The original cast of ONDINE included Margot Fonteyn (opposite) with Michael Somes as Palemon, the water nymph's doomed lover. Julia Farron appeared as Berta and Alexander Grant as Tirrenio, the Sea God. In the photographs Attilio Labis also appears as Palemon. ONDINE was the first substantial commissioned work which the distinguished young Westphalian composer, Hans Werner Henze, had ever undertaken in England, and the sets and costumes were designed by Lila de Nobili.

126

above: Annette Page, Rosemary Lindsay
opposite: Margot Fonteyn
below: Margot Fonteyn, Attilio Labis

"It's awfully difficult to persuade people how extra-ordinary Pavlova was. I don't think there's ever been a dancer like her, and there never will be now. When she came on to the stage she sent you wild with delight and she did have a very strong effect on Fred because she gave him his feeling for using every inch of the body to its extreme. She had marvellous abandon and she was totally pliable and she had this extraordinary electricity on stage."

WILLIAM CHAPPELL

131

above and opposite: Margot Fonteyn, Michael Somes

"I think that Frederick Ashton is one of the most theatrical of modern choreographers. His inspiration, as you know, was Pavlova, who was a marvellous dancer but also a wonderful entertainer. She was highly theatrical and he's never forgotten that. He's never forgotten its value or its impact on an audience. It wasn't that Pavlova tried to please the audience—it was just that she held them spellbound."

ALEXANDER GRANT

above: Margot Fonteyn
below: Leslie Edwards, Michael Somes, Margot Fonteyn, Alexander Grant
opposite: Alexander Grant
following page: Michael Somes, Margot Fonteyn

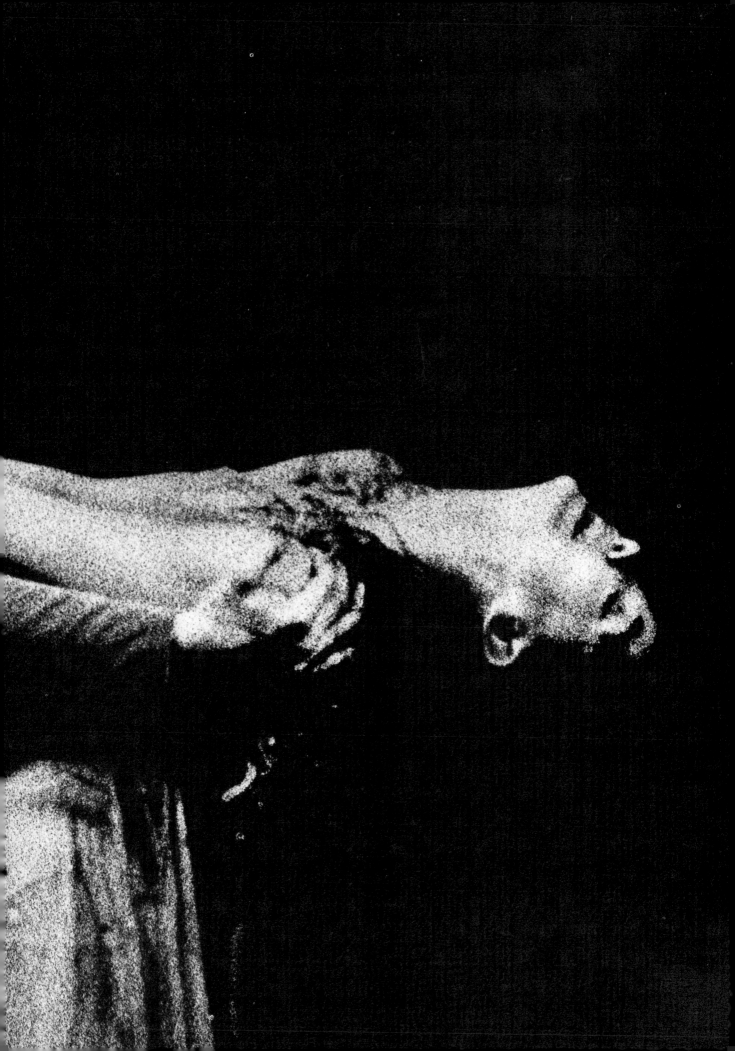

"Fred likes theatricality. I mean, he says he doesn't, but he's always the first person to catch on to the fact that you're theatrical and make use of it. On the other hand, he's also got X-ray eyes as far as performances go. He always sees and criticizes even the least trace of falseness. I think what he loved first about Margot Fonteyn was her disregard, or apparent disregard, for the public. She never involved herself in cheap fireworks and she never over-played. She despised tricks, and it was this which appealed to him first."

ROBERT HELPMANN

"I don't know what kind of dancer I would have been if Fred hadn't been there. I had a tremendous amount from him. No doubt there would have been other influences, but the company was so small and close knit before the war that we were together all the time, at rehearsals and in the canteen and on tour, and one was always with this very inspiring and interesting person. I think his influence on me is incalculable because of this."

MARGOT FONTEYN

"I would say about Fred that he did one thing that even Fokine and Massine didn't do. In LA FILLE MAL GARDÉE he created a pure classic, a real classical ballet which created what has become the English style of dancing. He has imprinted his own style on English dancers with that ballet."

MARIE RAMBERT

LA FILLE MAL GARDÉE

to music by Ferdinand Hérold
freely adapted and arranged by John Lanchbery

Frederick Ashton, although enormously inventive and original since the earliest days of his career, has always felt it his duty to preserve as well as innovate. The mixture of old and new, tradition and invention, is a constant feature of his work. The choreography of ONDINE included a direct reference, the shadow dance, to one of the nineteenth-century ballets about Ondine the water nymph, and in LA FILLE MAL GARDÉE, premièred in January, 1960, the long history of the work was very much part of Ashton's inspiration. Pavlova had danced a version of FILLE. Petipa and Ivanov had supervised its revival at the Maryinsky in 1885. The original creator of FILLE, Jean Bercher Daubeval, was a disciple and pupil of the great Jean Georges Noverre and its première, in 1789, had been a turning point in the history of ballet.

On a personal and choreographic level also, old and new came together in FILLE. It was Tamara Karsavina, whose career as a dancer had embraced the Maryinsky school and theatre, Fokine's first ballets for Diaghilev and the beginnings of Ballet Rambert, who encouraged Ashton to attempt it. "She kept saying that I ought to do it because it was such a marvellous subject and had marked the first entry of realism into ballet . . . She really sold it to me, and she taught me one of the mime scenes, where Lise dreams about having children. Choreographically it's all entirely mine except for that passage. Karsavina showed it to me in such an enchanting and marvellous way that I put it in straight away, just as she remembered it."

Everything which Ashton had ever learned about choreography, from whatever source, seems to have been put into practice in LA FILLE MAL GARDÉE; and it repaid the learning a hundredfold. FILLE is a sparkling, glowing ballet, the happiest and at times one of the most touching of all Ashton's works. Its two acts are so full of action, invention and fun that they reflect all his showmanship, his sense of humour, his gift for character through movement, and almost burst under the strain of the exciting dancing which fills them. It is also one of relatively few Ashton ballets which have been enthusiastically reviewed after the first performance. "So now I'm an Old Master," was his reported comment when he saw the newspapers.

The original cast of FILLE included Nadia Nerina (opposite) as Lise, Stanley Holden as her mother and David Blair as her lover. Alexander Grant played Alain, the rejected suitor, and Leslie Edwards played his father. The music which Ashton used for FILLE was not the music by Hertel which Pavlova and others had used. At short notice, John Lanchbery, the Principal Conductor of the Royal Ballet, undertook a complete and very successful reconstruction of the oldest musical version, by Ferdinand Hérold. The sets and costumes, by Osbert Lancaster, are also a major ingredient in the ballet's success. Their airy, rural quality seems to mirror everything that Ashton wanted. He has written: "There exists in my imagination a life in the country of eternally late spring, a leafy pastorale of perpetual sunshine and the humming of bees. . . . At some time or another, every artist pays his tribute to nature: my FILLE MAL GARDÉE is my poor man's Pastorale Symphony."

139

above: Alexander Grant, Leslie Edwards
opposite: Nadia Nerina, David Blair
following page: Alexander Grant

above: Stanley Holden, Nadia Nerina, David Blair
opposite: Stanley Holden, Leslie Edwards
following page: Nadia Nerina

"I think that ballet serves its purpose best when it evokes atmosphere. Possibly music could do the same by itself, but I think ballet adds a dimension in the evocation of an atmosphere or of a period. He can catch that like nobody else. It's wonderful, the way he can evoke the smell, the fragrance of a period and you get it in one. Take FILLE MAL GARDÉE. I really feel I'm in a French farmyard. Take NOCTURNE. In that one really felt one was in Paris in the dear, darling, gay Edwardian days. He has that way of absolutely getting hold of an atmosphere and making other people, like us dancers, get hold of it. He trained us all in that."

MICHAEL SOMES

"Which of his post-war ballets is most important? That's very hard. I'm torn between several. SYMPHONIC VARIATIONS, of course, but we've talked about that. I also think that FILLE MAL GARDÉE is a gem. It's not, after all, a question of whether a ballet is serious or not. For humour, for tenderness, for beautiful dancing, I think that FILLE takes a lot of beating. In FILLE and THE TWO PIGEONS he seems to get the whole period and style and to put on a wonderful display of sheer versatility in the choreography. I love those ballets. The music for both of them is unimportant, but I don't think that matters. He's got every ounce out of it. I think they're lovely ballets, perfect of their type."

NINETTE DE VALOIS

LES DEUX PIGEONS

LES DEUX PIGEONS

to music by André Messager

Frederick Ashton, who claims that choreographers often make bad teachers, has had little to do with the Royal Ballet School or its predecessors. Since he became Director, as he puts it, "the very young children are all submitted to me and I go to see the whole lot before they come in—sometimes it's miserable." But he is not a coach or a pedagogue, nor has he ever had the time or inclination to occupy himself with company classes or supervise routine rehearsals. His relationship with the Royal Ballet, to which he has devoted much of his creative life, has been expressed principally through each new work he choreographs. LA FILLE MAL GARDÉE and LES DEUX PIGEONS in particular epitomize the best qualities of the two Royal Ballet companies which helped to create them.

When preparing a new ballet in the rehearsal studio, Frederick Ashton works by an extraordinary, largely spontaneous, symbiotic process. He plans little in advance. Almost everything is worked out on the spot and Ashton, more than most choreographers, allows his ballets to be influenced by the characteristic qualities of his dancers, which he is very quick to recognize. It is this which gives his choreography its special, unforced fluency, and this also which makes him strongly prefer to work with dancers he knows well. He confesses to a sense of unease when he works abroad, or with a ballet company he does not know intimately. He also, as we have seen, dislikes second casts.

Ashton's ballets for the Sadlers Wells Theatre Ballet, re-styled the touring section of the Royal Ballet in 1956 and merged with the main company in 1970, show the speed with which he can adjust to unfamiliar conditions and dancers who are relative strangers. LES DEUX PIGEONS, premièred in February, 1961, is a youthful, joyful ballet, just like LA FILLE MAL GARDÉE. But LES DEUX PIGEONS has the freshness of FILLE without its sharp and diamond-brilliant glitter. It is softer toned, about romance as well as love, a revealing dialogue of two young people who quarrel, separate and re-unite. Neither the lovers nor the gipsies who tempt one of them away have names or much dramatic stuffing, and the background, Bohemian Paris, is a cliché. But the dancing is never hackneyed or anything but alive. Even the music comes over freshly in the context of Ashton's choreography.

LES DEUX PIGEONS is, like LA FILLE MAL GARDÉE, a two-act ballet. Since 1958, Ashton has preferred two acts to three for his occasional long ballets because, as he once complained, "by the end of the second act the story has usually petered out anyway". LES DEUX PIGEONS is loosely based on La Fontaine's fable of the same name and it retains some links with Mérante's nineteenth-century ballet on Messager's music and the same theme. But, as the critic of *The Financial Times* wrote, this ballet "is not an old tale retold but a new one newly felt, newly imagined in terms of movement . . .". The original cast included Lynn Seymour (opposite) and Christopher Gable (who replaced the injured Donald Britton), with Elizabeth Anderton as the gipsy girl. The décor and costumes are by Jacques Dupont.

154

"Fred is wonderfully musical, with just the right kind of musicality for a choreographer or a dancer. He doesn't slavishly follow a score; he has just that little bit of waywardness with the music. He hears a rhythm or a mood which perhaps not even the composer intended. He adds to it and brings out things which aren't obvious. It's always very exciting and he always treats the music sympathetically, but quite without false reverence."

MICHAEL SOMES

above: Johaar Mosaval
below: Christopher Gable
opposite: Lynn Seymour, Christopher Gable

above, below, opposite: Christopher Gable, Lynn Seymour

"How does he start to work? He listens to a lot of pieces
of music and he has a feeling for one piece at one moment.
Somebody perhaps suggests something to him and it isn't
something he feels like doing at that time. But then he
changes, all kinds of things happen, and there comes a
day when that piece of music inspires him and he wants
to do it. In that way, he's instinctive—he does what he
feels is right and he doesn't like to rationalize too much.
One often said, 'Fred, why don't you do another ballet?'
And he would just reply, 'Oh, it's so difficult . . . I can't
find any music that I want to do.' He has to wait until
something comes along and he feels sure. That's why he's
so great and why he goes on being great—because he
hasn't formed himself some image of what he ought to
be: he just goes on instinctively doing what seems right."

MARGOT FONTEYN

PERSEPHONE

by André Gide
to music by Igor Stravinsky

"Consciously, all through my career, I have been working to make the ballet independent of literary and pictorial motives. . . . If the ballet is to survive, it must survive through its dancing qualities . . . it is the dance that *must* be paramount."
These words are as much a 'credo' as any of Frederick Ashton's rare writings about choreography. Not all his ballets, or even most, have been innocent of literary and pictorial associations nor does he claim that great ballets cannot be based on literary themes. But he practises a rigorous self-discipline when he makes this sort of material into ballet. He pares whatever he can out of an elaborate libretto before he uses it and he prefers to take his lead directly from the music. Even when he is not able to restrict the libretto to "the merest thread of an idea which can be ignored", this is still true. He can detect and make use of every undercurrent or nuance of any music which he seeks out and uses for a ballet. His mother's musical inclinations, and Constant Lambert's tuition, may have helped to develop this arcane talent, which is one of his outstanding strengths as a choreographer. It is the fertility and inventiveness of the ideas which Ashton finds in music that characterize his very best works.
The most striking feature of PERSEPHONE, which makes it unique among ballets, is that the title role is spoken as well as danced. This unusual idea can be traced back to the influence, and shortcomings, of the "mysterious, extravagant, biblical Rubinstein", whom Diaghilev originally discovered. In 1934, five years after Ashton's spell with the Ballets Ida Rubinstein and long after her break with Diaghilev's Ballets Russes, Ida Rubinstein was the centrepiece of the first production, in Paris, of the Stravinsky/Gide 'mélodrame' which she had commissioned. But the production was not successful, nor was the collaboration a happy one. Stravinsky's musical setting demanded that words and syllables of Gide's verse libretto be distorted and protracted out of all recognition and Gide bitterly resented this approach. The difference of opinion is said to have made this collaboration the least happy of Stravinsky's life.
Nevertheless, PERSEPHONE shows traces of these difficulties only in apparent clashes of intention. The music and the words seem to attempt different tasks. In his ballet, premièred in December, 1961, Ashton followed the dictates of the music. *The Times'* critic wrote: "We had begun to give Ashton a place among inventive but essentially decorative choreographers; PERSEPHONE has inspired him to a vital and pugnacious originality of invention. . . . The heavy, garish décors of Nico Ghika set the seal on a version of PERSEPHONE which is more Russian than Greek or French, more savage and pagan than classic or Christian."
Despite respectful reviews, Ashton's elaborate PERSEPHONE and its French libretto did not find favour with London audiences. The work had few performances. In the original and only cast, Svetlana Beriosova (opposite) persuasively combined a ballerina's role and an actress's delivery of Gide's verses and she was joined by Keith Rosson as Pluto, Gerd Larsen as Demeter and Alexander Grant as Mercury. Derek Rencher played Demophoön, Persephone's lover.

below: Pamela Moncur, Christine Beckley, Svetlana Beriosova
Georgina Parkinson, Laura Connor
opposite: Svetlana Beriosova

above and opposite: Keith Rosson, Svetlana Beriosova

"It's always the music that starts me off. The story doesn't count at all, though I suppose that if I found an absolutely superb story I might commission somebody to write the music. Usually I just hear a piece of music and I do that."

FREDERICK ASHTON

above: Svetlana Beriosova

"I don't think that the audience has ever entered into it at all with him. I think that he has a sort of Olympian aloofness to the audience but he gets terribly worried and frightfully hurt and spiky when he has a bad review. The critics, after all, have been rather censorious all along the line and it's only as his new ballets are given more and more that they're accepted and become classics and those who criticized them initially say that they're masterpieces."

CECIL BEATON

above: Gerd Larsen, Alexander Grant
below: Svetlana Beriosova, Derek Rencher

"Fred's like all really creative people. He gets in a terrible state of panic almost every time he does something new and he likes to come to me and ask if it's going to be all right. I once said 'No, it's not,' and he didn't do that ballet. He likes to ask his close friends for their advice because we know what he's done and what he's good at. He doesn't always take notice, not if he's sure. It's when he's not sure that he listens."

WILLIAM CHAPPELL

175

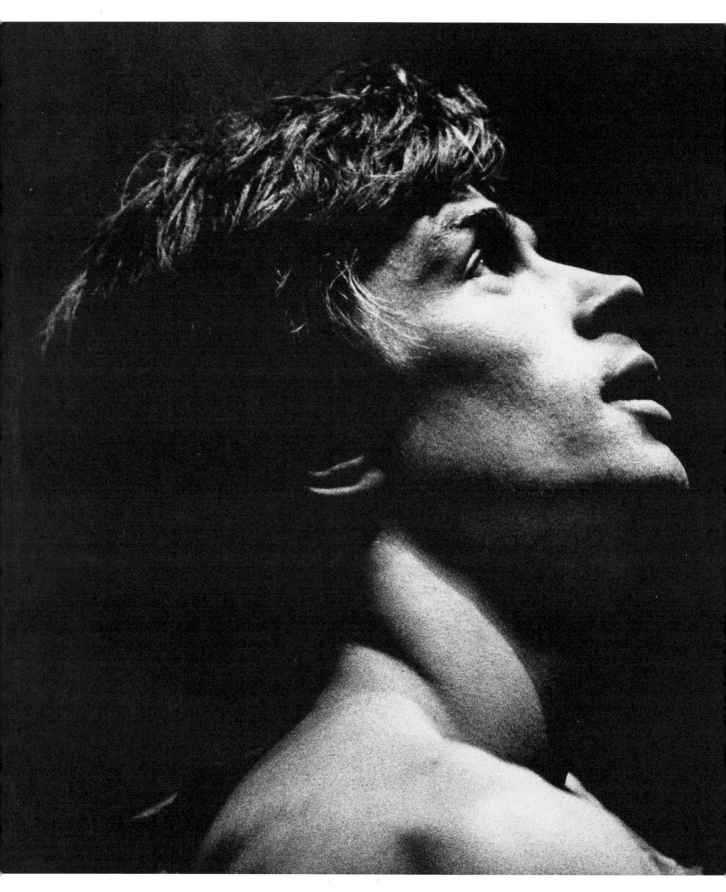

above: Rudolf Nureyev

MARGUERITE AND ARMAND

to music by Franz Liszt

During the 1950s the prevailing critical attitude to Ashton's ballets was one of lukewarm sympathy. The London critics understood what he was doing but failed to see the necessity for him to do it. At the beginning of the sixties even his less successful works were greeted with rapture. One reason for this sudden re-appraisal was his new-found independence of Margot Fonteyn. "LA FILLE MAL GARDÉE," wrote *The Guardian*'s critic on 30 August, 1962, "showed for the first time . . . that he [Ashton] did not depend on Fonteyn as his interpreter . . . he, almost as much as the ballet public, needed this sign of self-sufficiency."

MARGUERITE AND ARMAND, premièred in March, 1963, is the last ballet which Frederick Ashton choreographed for Margot Fonteyn. It is not a major work and it is often regarded just as a vehicle for its two superstars, Fonteyn and Nureyev. But it is hardly ever safe to dismiss an Ashton ballet quite that easily. MARGUERITE AND ARMAND is also a very individual, rather surprising ballet, with many echoes of Ashton's work in the thirties. Liszt was one of Constant Lambert's favourite composers. APPARITIONS (1936) combined music by Liszt, Margot Fonteyn's dancing and Cecil Beaton's décor and costumes. It seems almost like a trick of perspective or an optical illusion that MARGUERITE AND ARMAND is so similar in specification.

One of Frederick Ashton's complaints about his years at an English public school is that they made him very careful. From that time on, he says, he has been a little withdrawn and guarded, somewhat inclined to conceal his most revealing characteristics. In choreography his classicism has often shielded a romantic imagination from notice. Romance colours much of what he does, but it has rarely been the keynote. MARGUERITE AND ARMAND, based on *La Dame Aux Camélias* by Alexandre Dumas, broke this rule and many others when it was prèmiered. It is a highly romantic ballet, full of fevered flash-backs and outpourings of passion. Only the pace at which it moves prevents it becoming self-indulgent or cloying. The dancing is so hectic that one is protected from the plushy romanticism of *La Traviata* as well as wholly insulated from reality. "It's a bit the result of *Marienbad*, you know," said Frederick Ashton to *The Observer*, "I loved that film. Resnais could make a marvellous *Camélia*."

In October, 1963, in the aftermath of MARGUERITE AND ARMAND, Frederick Ashton was interviewed by *The Times*: "I dislike a star system," he said, "although I do not necessarily dislike stars." Certainly his search for a ballet for Margot Fonteyn and her new partner, Rudolf Nureyev, had gone on for a long time. He was already looking for the right idea and piece of music in May, 1961. He settled on Liszt's B minor Piano Sonata, orchestrated first by Humphrey Searle and later by Gordon Jacob, after hearing it unexpectedly on the radio in April, 1962.

MARGUERITE AND ARMAND, which was a qualified critical success when it was first shown, has been an enormous box-office success throughout its life. If ONDINE was Ashton's final tribute to Fonteyn the dancer, MARGUERITE AND ARMAND is a tribute to her enormous skill as an actress and to her appeal to the ballet public. It is her showpiece, as it is Nureyev's. In the original cast, Michael Somes, as Armand's father, created an outstanding cameo role of severity and sympathy combined.

177

above and opposite: Rudolf Nureyev, Margot Fonteyn

above: Cecil Beaton, Frederick Ashton, Margot Fonteyn
opposite: Margot Fonteyn, Rudolf Nureyev

"I think that when he starts to work on a ballet his one idea is that it will be a marvellous means of his creating something that is within the reach of his particular idiom. With MARGUERITE AND ARMAND he heard this Liszt on the radio and it came to him like a vision. Each section of the music seems to mean a different phase in the story of Camille and it led up to her death and it was ideal. And when the music finished, he rang up the B.B.C. to find exactly what it was they'd played. That was his moment of illumination."

CECIL BEATON

"I don't feel he'll ever run out. He gets his thin patches and he gets his lazy patches. He doesn't like working with lots of people, especially now, but I can't blame him for that. And if there's some ghastly 'corps de ballet' number and no one knows how they get out of it and into something else he leaves it and we make it work. I help him, we all help him. We try and leave as much energy as possible for him to create."

MICHAEL SOMES

opposite: Rudolf Nureyev

following page: Margot Fonteyn, Rudolf Nureyev

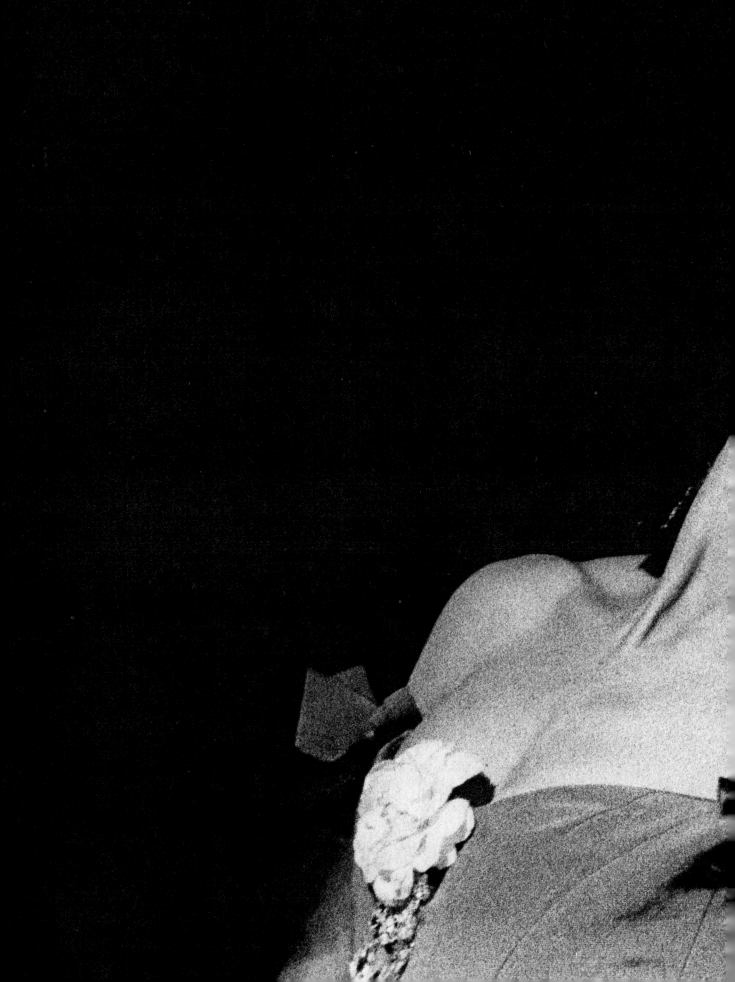

above: Margot Fonteyn, Michael Somes
opposite and following: Rudolf Nureyev, Margot Fonteyn

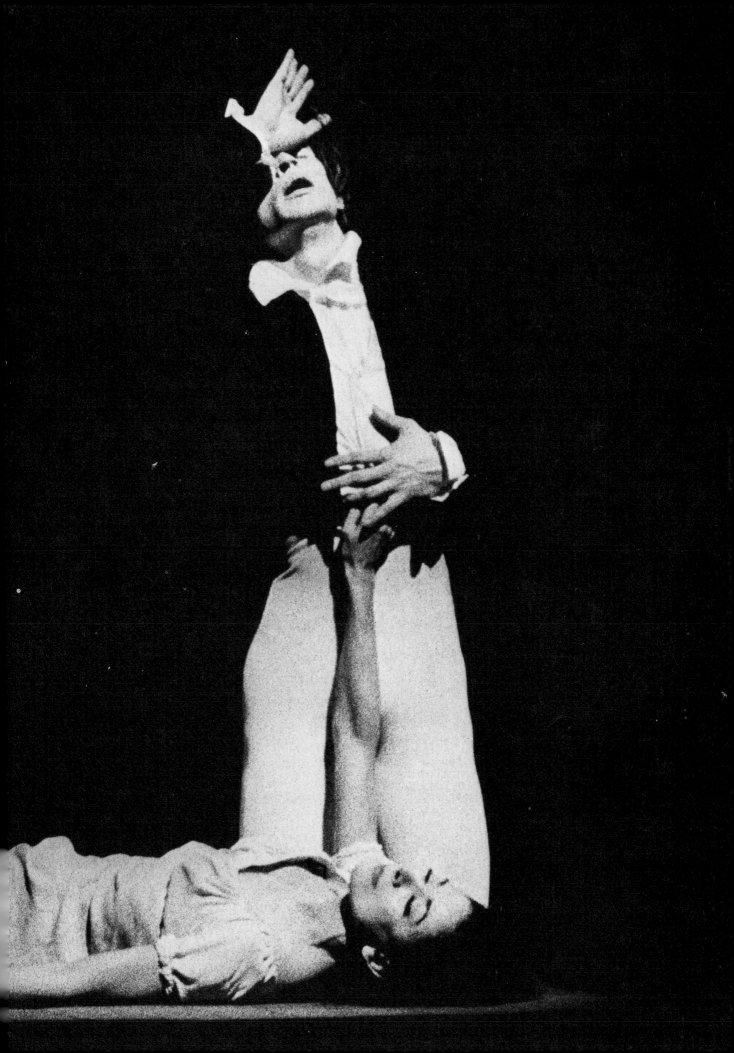

"I am accused of favouring the boys—the little boys, the big boys, all the boys. And I cannot help it because to my mind when a boy at an ordinary school in any part of England makes the decision to become a ballet dancer, he must have a real vocation. With a girl, it means nothing. Everybody thinks it would be much nicer for her to go to the Royal Ballet School than to become a secretary. But the boys very often make this decision with their fathers and their headmasters in direct opposition and amidst the jeers and cries of half the schoolboys. I think it's very touching and I'm out to help all I can. Because there's something else too. Whenever I'm lecturing I always say to people 'Don't you realize that the history of ballet is the history of the male dancer and the male choreographer?' It has nothing to do with women except in a secondary role. It's only when the whole thing's come down to nothing that women become the best pioneer workers. They make the best secretaries, for the same reason. But once ballet's got to a certain level again it's got to be handed back to the men."

NINETTE DE VALOIS

THE DREAM

to music by Felix Mendelssohn-Bartholdy

"It is probably no accident," wrote Clive Barnes in 1961, "that both Ashton and Balanchine are attached to permanent ballet companies, backed by permanent ballet schools. There has been a rhythm and order to their careers as one successive generation of dancers has succeeded the next, and ballet seasons lap over them like waves. . ."
Although Ninette de Valois was the original architect and inspiration of the Vic-Wells, Sadlers Wells and Royal Ballets, Frederick Ashton contributed enormously to their artistic development over the years. When de Valois retired, in August, 1963, he chose to play a major organizational role as well. "I've probably enjoyed being Director more than I think," he says, "my passion is to maintain Ninette's standards and have the Royal Ballet accepted as a really great company."
It is always possible, even likely, that an artist who also serves as an administrator will find it very much more difficult to practise his art successfully. Frederick Ashton likes to spend time simply thinking about his plans for ballets. He works intensively and quickly on new ballets but he recuperates at leisure, during long periods of unenergetic rumination. As Director he has not had this opportunity. Between 1948 and the end of 1960 Ashton produced five full length ballets as well as one-act ballets and minor works. In the ten years since 1960 he has not attempted a new full length ballet and he has only created a limited number of shorter works.
However, Ashton has neither dried up nor, his real fear, repeated himself, since he became Director of the Royal Ballet. THE DREAM is a one-act ballet which shows him at his very best. Choreographed in 1964, for the celebrations of the four hundredth anniversary of William Shakespeare's birth, THE DREAM was the first ballet that Ashton created after becoming Director. If this makes it sound a little formal, like the 'pièces d'occasion' at which Ashton is particularly skilful, the work itself belies this. It is very Shakespearian, but Ashton was evidently not overawed by his responsibilities to Shakespeare. His version of Bottom's dream represents the spirit of Arden and not just the action of Shakespeare's play. The comedy and the incidents survive but the regal, beautiful, half-sinister fairies, Titania and Oberon, are wonderfully well characterized in Ashton's ballet. In these two roles Ashton seems to have caught everything essential to his (and Shakespeare's) vision.
Oberon and Titania in THE DREAM were first danced by Anthony Dowell and Antoinette Sibley (opposite). They were the first major roles that Ashton created for these two dancers and his choreography not only did them justice in 1964 but somehow, presciently, hinted at their great achievements together since then. In the original cast they were joined by Alexander Grant, as Bottom (opposite), and Keith Martin, as Puck. But the ballet has been successful since it was premièred with many casts and in many places. In the photographs the 'rude mechanicals' are played by members of the touring section of the Royal Ballet led by Ronald Emblem. The sets and costumes were designed by Henry Bardon and David Walker.

192

above: Antoinette Sibley, Anthony Dowell

above: Anthony Dowell
below: Alexander Grant
opposite and following: Anthony Dowell and Antoinette Sibley

MONOTONES

to music by Erik Satie

Since Diaghilev's death, it has become the custom for choreographers to control and supervise all the elements of a ballet in the making. The sets and costumes of a new ballet, and its music, are now created to the choreographer's specification and not to the dictates of a third party. It is a change which Ninette de Valois, among others, regrets. She considers that too much strain can be placed upon the choreographer by the requirements of production as well as choreography. "Fred," she says, "is, for example, very kind to his designers—sometimes too kind, sometimes to his own disadvantage. He lets things go by which perhaps he should have thought out more thoroughly. I think there has got to be someone outside, who can be slightly ruthless over this sort of question and who can help the choreographer along."

Frederick Ashton's ballets have over the years been criticized more often and more severely for defects in the décor and costumes than for shortcomings in the casting or choreography. It is the design side which is nearly always weakest. Ashton has an acute sense of the visual in his private life and he expresses himself very individually and very exactly in the way that he arranges 'objets' in the living room of his home and carefully nurtures shaped hedgerows in his country garden. But in selecting and commissioning designers for his ballets, his eye is never as sharp as one expects. He approaches the whole problem with diffidence, as if he hesitated to impose his own ideas on a professional designer and it may be, as Cecil Beaton suggests, that he is not always clear about what he wants at the stage when the designs must be made final. Ashton's characteristic way of working is to eliminate. "Usually as I work I just reject and reject," he says, "and I purify everything and get to the essence of what I really want." This method, ideal for choreography, has not always seemed to work so well for his designers.

MONOTONES II, choreographed in 1965, and MONOTONES I, choreographed in 1966, are short companion ballets in which Ashton's genius for elimination is of the essence. Neither ballet has a set. Instead, probing spot lights isolate the dancers from their surroundings and cushion them from mundane considerations of place and time, and both trios of dancers, two men and a girl in MONOTONES II and one man and two girls in MONOTONES I, are dressed in body stockings and simple head-dresses which Frederick Ashton designed. It is the only occasion that he has designed costumes for one of his own ballets.

MONOTONES I and II are performed together, as one ballet. But they are not closely similar, though both are among Ashton's best works. The music for MONOTONES II is other-worldly and the choreography is cool, lyrical and very beautiful. MONOTONES I is earthier, coarser, less perfect and therefore less detached. But even MONOTONES II always reminds us of Ashton's humanity and his concern for events and people round him. It is not abstract in the sense of being dry, arid, inhuman or lacking in warmth. Very much the opposite. Only if either part of MONOTONES ever had a theme or story, no trace survives in the choreography.

The original cast of MONOTONES II (opposite) consisted of Anthony Dowell, Vyvyan Lorrayne and Robert Mead. MONOTONES I was danced first by Georgian Parkinson, Ann Jenner and Brian Shaw.

201

202

above: Anthony Dowell, Vyvyan Lorrayne, Robert Mead

below: Georgina Parkinson, Ann Jenner, Brian Shaw

JAZZ CALENDAR
to music by Richard Rodney Bennett

> Monday's child is fair of face,
> Tuesday's child is full of grace,
> Wednesday's child is full of woe,
> Thursday's child has far to go,
> Friday's child is loving and giving,
> Saturday's child works hard for his living
> And the child that is born on the Sabbath day
> Is bonny and blithe, and good and gay.

During Ashton's years as Director of the Royal Ballet, Nijinska, Balanchine, Tudor, Bruhn, Cranko, Nureyev, and McMillan mounted revivals or created new ballets for the company. At some stages, their efforts and the classics monopolized the seven performances per fortnight which the Royal Ballet then enjoyed in London, and Ashton's own opportunities to work as choreographer were cut to the bone as a result. The sixties were a curious mixture for Frederick Ashton. On the one hand he did some of his best work. On the other hand he did relatively little, much of it on a small scale, and he was criticized for the deliberately outmoded flavour of new works which, like LA FILLE MAL GARDÉE, LES DEUX PIGEONS and THE DREAM, contained stylistic and scenic references back to the nineteenth century. Frederick Ashton was knighted for services to ballet in 1962 and he became Director of the Royal Ballet in 1963. In 1964, Clive Barnes suggested in the *Spectator* that he should be "saved for the nation" from choreographic inactivity. JAZZ CALENDAR, with SINFONIETTA (1967) and MONOTONES, was Ashton's proof that he was neither an inactive volcano nor a national monument.

JAZZ CALENDAR, based on a picturesque children's rhyme and a jazzy score which allows the prominent members of the Royal Ballet a memorable 'divertissement' each, is, like some latter-day FAÇADE, witty and piquant, "not only a good ballet but a good joke too", as *The Times* commented. When asked about the part that humour plays in his ballets, Frederick Ashton is always careful to emphasize the craftsmanship with which it needs to be underpinned. "You've always got to bear in mind," he says, "that there might be an audience who didn't think the ballet was the least bit funny. The dance has to be decent in itself." JAZZ CALENDAR is carefully and skilfully constructed, and although the music is weak its shortcomings have never prevented JAZZ CALENDAR stopping the show. It is one of Ashton's greatest recent favourites, with the Royal Opera House audience and even with the critics. Only in America has it been anything less than successful.

The original cast of JAZZ CALENDAR included Vergie Derman (opposite) as Monday; Robert Mead, Merle Park and Anthony Dowell as Tuesday; Vyvyan Lorrayne and others as Wednesday; Alexander Grant and others as Thursday; Antoinette Sibley and Rudolf Nureyev as Friday; Desmond Doyle and others as Saturday and Marilyn Trounson and the entire cast as Sunday. JAZZ CALENDAR is as much a show piece for the company as LES PATINEURS, LES RENDEZVOUS and the other Ashton 'lollipops' were in their time. Perhaps it will last as long. The costumes and décor were designed by Derek Jarman.

above: Robert Mead, Merle Park, Anthony Dowell
below: Vyvyan Lorrayne

above and below: Rudolf Nureyev
and Antoinette Sibley

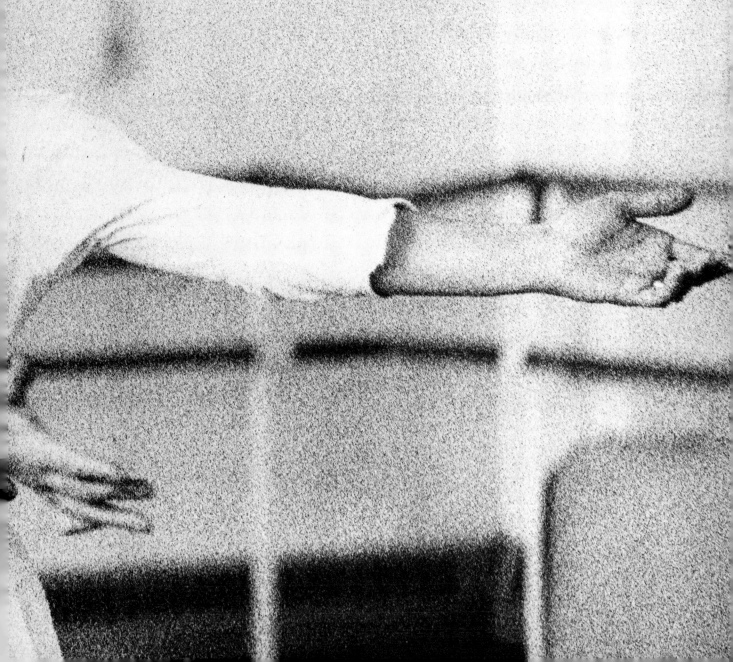

ENIGMA VARIATIONS

ENIGMA VARIATIONS

to music by Edward Elgar

In London during the 1920s, Frederick Ashton saw almost all the new ballets given by the Diaghilev company. "All those productions," he says, "certainly had a profound effect upon me. I cherish them particularly and I feel that it's important that people should see this as part of their dancing heritage."

Frederick Ashton's homage to the dancing heritage has been expressed by the revivals of LES NOCES and LES BICHES, which he inspired, by the care with which he has restored and refreshed tired productions of the classics, and by direct reference to the works of other choreographers which he has, on occasion, incorporated into his ballets. He cherishes the dancing heritage and he takes care to preserve what he regards as worth while from his own works. Particular movements and styles of movement are not forgotten. Particular themes and pieces of music have been re-used.

His retentive, eclectic quality as an artist shows itself also in the history of this ballet; the ENIGMA VARIATIONS are among the best and best known of Edward Elgar's works and Julia Trevelyan Oman, who designed Ashton's ballet, first suggested the music to him while she was still a student at art school. At that time Ashton rejected the suggestion. But he revived the project in 1966 and premièred his ballet in 1968. The idea had been buried—stored—but not forgotten.

In the ENIGMA VARIATIONS Edward Elgar, working with almost child-like pleasure in his own ingenuity, concealed musical portraits of his friends and family as well as the still unsolvable enigma. As a result, the music is a storehouse of interest for the choreographer. In 1940 Frank Staff mounted an abstract ballet on this music and in Ashton's hands it became the basis for a masterpiece. Edward Elgar is the most English of composers. The period when he wrote was the heyday of an England to which Ashton, among many others, looks back with some nostalgia. In more than one way Frederick Ashton was able to discover special resources in himself through dealing with Elgar's life and work.

Ashton's ballet is effective on a variety of levels. It offers comical and sometimes rousing portraits of Elgar's "Friends Pictured Within". It is a resonant and telling evocation of the period in late Victorian times when Elgar wrote. It contains a moving description of the relations between Elgar, his wife and August Jaeger. But above all it is a personal statement, Ashton's reconstruction of the hopes and artistic aspirations which Elgar attached to the ENIGMA VARIATIONS. It is this which gives it depth as well as charm, human sympathy as well as vitality.

In the original cast Svetlana Beriosova (opposite) appeared as Lady Elgar and Derek Rencher as the composer, with Desmond Doyle as Jaeger. Antoinette Sibley created the role of Dorabella and Anthony Dowell made a brief and fiery appearance as Troyte Griffith. The cast also included Stanley Holden, Brian Shaw, Alexander Grant, Robert Mead, Vyvyan Lorrayne, Georgina Parkinson, Wayne Sleep, Leslie Edwards, and Deanne Bergsma. Elgar's music was changed in only one particular for Ashton's production. The finale, describing the composer himself, was restored to the short and brilliant form in which Elgar originally presented it to the public and the grandiose climax which Elgar eventually substituted was not employed.

opposite (above): Vyvyan Lorrayne, Robert Mead, Stanley Holden
opposite (below): Anthony Dowell
left: Georgina Parkinson
below: Desmond Doyle, Svetlana Beriosova, Derek Rencher

above: Brian Shaw, Robert Mead, Stanley Holden, Anthony Dowell
Alexander Grant, Desmond Doyle, Wayne Sleep

above: Desmond Doyle, Svetlana Beriosova, Derek Rencher
opposite: Derek Rencher, Antoinette Sibley

LAMENT OF THE WAVES

LAMENT OF THE WAVES

to music by Gérard Masson

Even Frederick Ashton's very earliest ballets, for Marie Rambert or at the Trocadero for C. B. Cochran, are said to have demonstrated that he owed his allegiance to the classical techniques and style of dancing. This, of all the features of his work is the longest lasting, most significant, most basic characteristic. "I always return to Petipa over everything," he says, "people sometimes find me at a matinée of THE SLEEPING BEAUTY, which I have seen literally hundreds of times. And they ask me what I'm doing and I say 'having a private lesson'. I watch the marvellous way that he handles the people and the crowds and builds up to a climax and all that sort of thing. I'm not looking at the dancers at all. I'm looking at the way that he achieves the effects that he's after. That fascinates me."

During the Second World War, with works like DANTE SONATA, Ashton seems to have felt his way towards a more explicit, though not necessarily less classical, style of choreography. Although few of those ballets have survived, he learned, in Michael Somes' view, all sorts of new ways of using the body at that period. These techniques came in useful even when the ballets for which he'd conceived them were forgotten, and his post-war ballets, especially SYMPHONIC VARIATIONS, show a new freedom and assurance, a new ability to let emotion illuminate and moderate classical dancing.

Ballets like LAMENT OF THE WAVES confirm Ashton's ability to mint classicism afresh when it is necessary. LAMENT OF THE WAVES was the last ballet that Frederick Ashton choreographed for the London-based Royal Ballet company before he completed his term as its Director. It was premièred in February, 1970 and it is one of his most individual recent works. The choice of music, theme and dancers confirm what is probably the strongest impression of Ashton's last ten years with the Royal Ballet. He has not dried up, or even faltered, as a result of losing his close creative ties with Margot Fonteyn, growing older and taking on an increasing burden of administrative responsibility. Each young dancer who catches his eye and each contemporary change of mood which impresses him is taken into account in his work. LAMENT is full of challenging images and of activity. How does he continue to take so much in and pour so much out? The scenario of LAMENT OF THE WAVES is very simple and very brief: "Two young lovers are drowned." The lovers, created by Marilyn Trounson and Carl Myers (opposite), re-enact and mourn for the unexpected loss of their young lives in a 'pas de deux' which is among the longest, most intense and most adventurous imaginable. The music, by a young French composer, is twice interrupted by aleatoric mutterings from the members of the orchestra, who say their names and the names of the instruments they play. But it is as deeply evocative of the patterns and rhythms of the sea as Henze's score for ONDINE, which also brought out the best in Ashton. In LAMENT the two young dancers explore poses and movements of extraordinary vitality and finally, menaced by an urchin-like creature of inner space succumb not charmingly or romantically but painfully, gasping for breath and life. The ballet has an oblique, intangible and disturbing quality about it. It leaves a thoughtful aftertaste. The critics enjoyed it, on the whole, rather more than some of the audiences.

right and below: Frederick Ashton
Marilyn Trounson, Carl Myers

"I have no hesitation in saying that in the artistic sense, Frederick Ashton has influenced more dancers, even those who have had no connection with him, than any other person, Pavlova and Balanchine included. The others tell you what to do and you either can or can't do it. But he teaches people to use themselves and their own bodies and minds."

MICHAEL SOMES

FAÇADE

to music by William Walton

Besides being one of the funniest Ashton ballets, FAÇADE is also the oldest in any current repertoire. It has links with almost every stage of Ashton's career. "I first heard it just as an entertainment," he says, "That was in Paris, when I was with Ida Rubinstein. I thought at the time what a marvellous ballet it would make."

FAÇADE was premièred by the Camargo Society, the midwife of British ballet, and it was revived at the Ballet Club, and re-produced and re-designed for Sadlers Wells in 1940. It has been in the repertoire ever since. "I always look back with particular pleasure upon FAÇADE," says Ashton, "because I really liked that collaboration with William Walton. It was a marvellous score by any standards and I had a marvellous cast for it and it was the first ballet that I'd done bringing humour into a piece that was classically based. I still do regard it as a rather particular landmark in my work."

It is unusual for Frederick Ashton to speak emphatically about any ballet other than a new one. "It doesn't worry me," he says, "whether my ballets will live or not. One just does not know, and the repertoire of a ballet company that is alive and progressing shouldn't be cluttered with too many works by one choreographer. Those that are tough, and they may not be my best works, will survive. Something like FILLE will live, because it's loose enough to give everybody their own interpretation. But a ballet like SYMPHONIC VARIATIONS could just be a mess in the end, if it's not quite perfect."

To write about Frederick Ashton is to write about the history of British ballet. With Ninette de Valois and Marie Rambert, he is its founder. On 24 July, 1970, the Gala Performance at the Royal Opera House was in honour of Ashton's retirement from the Directorship of the Royal Ballet. It included thirty-seven items and reminded us of forty years of his choreography. FAÇADE, SYMPHONIC VARIATIONS and LA FILLE MAL GARDÉE were among its highlights, three great ballets, each reminiscent of a distinctive part of Ashton's career and each a lasting proof of his great and varied talent. From A TRAGEDY OF FASHION to LAMENT OF THE WAVES and THE CREATURES OF PROMETHEUS. From Massine's school, the Ballet Club and the Camargo Society to the Directorship of the Royal Ballet. A long journey, and the present summit may not mark the end of Ashton's progress. "Sometimes," says Cecil Beaton, "when I was designing for Fred I said 'Well, are you satisfied with this?' And he would say 'Yes.' But there was always a little doubt in his voice. I think he always feels that something could be better or something is being missed." "I think it is the sign of a true artist," said Tamara Karsavina in a radio programme about Ashton, "always to want something higher that is out of reach, always to think to himself that he could do better."

"He has found the administrative side of being Director of the Royal Ballet," says Robert Helpmann, "as boring as he used to find class in the old days. I think that he feels that it is drying him up because he lacks the time he needs to create. He's resigning his position as Director to do what he bloody well should be doing. And that is making ballets."

above: Douglas Steuart, Diana Vere, Leslie
      Edwards, Ann Jenner in FAÇADE
below: Jennifer Penney in FAÇADE
opposite: Merle Park, Alexander Grant in FAÇADE

above: Jennifer Penney in LE BAISER DE LA FÉE
opposite: Rudolf Nureyev in LES RENDEZVOUS

"His greatest ballet? I couldn't possibly tell you. You could say which was the most difficult achievement. Perhaps that was his greatest. Or you could say the simplest little ballet he ever did, where he made the most out of the least—I don't know how you judge the greatest. It depends on what you like."

MICHAEL SOMES

below and opposite: Margot Fonteyn, Rudolf Nureyev in APPARITIONS

1959—May 7

LES RENDEZVOUS
(New production—Royal Opera House, for Royal Ballet)

M: Auber/Lambert *D:* Sophie Fedorovitch (décor only—Act 1 of sets originally made for "La Traviata") and William Chappell

Cast: *Amoureux* Nadia Nerina, Brian Shaw, *Pas de Trois* Merle Park, Petrus Bosman, Graham Usher

See above (1933, 1937, 1947, 1956)

1959—November 26

RÊVE D'AMOUR—Pas de Deux from **RAYMONDA**
(Theatre Royal, Drury Lane, for Royal Academy of Dancing Gala)

M: Alexander Glazunov *D:* Leslie Hurry

Cast: Margot Fonteyn, Michael Somes

1960—January 28

LA FILLE MAL GARDÉE
(Royal Opera House, for Royal Ballet)

A: Jean Dauberval *M:* Ferdinand Hérold *arr:* John Lanchbery *D:* Osbert Lancaster

Cast: *Widow Simone* Stanley Holden, *Lise* Nadia Nerina, *Colas* David Blair, *Thomas* Leslie Edwards, *Alain* Alexander Grant, *A Village Notary* Franklin White, *His Secretary* Maurice Metliss, *Cockerel and Hens* Laurence Ruffell, Margaret Lyons, Robin Haig, Maureen Maitland, Gloria Bluemel, *Friends of Lise* Christine Beckley, Shirley Grahame, Vyvyan Lorrayne, Georgina Parkinson, Debra Wayne, Audrey Henderson, Monica Mason, Doreen Eastlake, *Boy with Flute* John Sale, with corps de ballet

1960—March 1

SCÈNE D'AMOUR from **RAYMONDA**
(Royal Opera House, for Ballet Royal)

M: Glazunov *D:* Hurry

Cast: Fonteyn, Somes

See above (1959)

1961—February 14

LES DEUX PIGEONS
(Royal Opera House, for Royal Ballet)

M: André Messager *D:* Jacques Dupont

Cast: *The Young Girl* Lynn Seymour, *The Young Man* Christopher Gable, *His Mother* Shirley Bishop, *The Gypsy Girl* Elizabeth Anderton, *Her Lover* Robert Mead, *A Gypsy Boy* Johaar Mosaval, with corps de ballet

1961—December 12

PERSEPHONE
(Royal Opera House, for Royal Ballet)

A: André Gide *M:* Igor Stravinsky *D:* Nico Ghika

Cast: *Persephone* Svetlana Beriosova, *Mercury* Alexander Grant, *Pluto* Keith Rosson, *Demeter* Gerd Larsen, *Demaphoön* Derek Rencher, *Eumolpus* Andre Turp (tenor), *Persephone's Friends* Georgina Parkinson, Christine Beckley, Monica Mason, Audrey Farriss, Pamela Moncur, *Hours* Deanne Bergsma, Vyvyan Lorrayne, Betty Kavanagh, Rosalind Eyre, Louanne Richards, Heather Clipperton, with corps de ballet

1962—May 3

Pas de Deux, Variations and Coda from **RAYMONDA** (Royal Opera House, for Royal Ballet)

M: Alexander Glazunov *D:* André Levasseur

Cast: Svetlana Beriosova, Donald MacLeary

See above (1959, 1960)

1963—March 12

MARGUERITE AND ARMAND
(Royal Opera House, for Royal Ballet)

A: after "The Lady of the Camellias" by Alexander Dumas *D:* Cecil Beaton *M:* Prelude and Sonata in B minor by Franz Liszt *orch:* Humphrey Searle

Cast: *Marguerite* Margot Fonteyn, *Armand* Rudolf Nureyev, *His Father* Michael Somes, *A Duke* Leslie Edwards, *Admirers* Keith Rosson, Bryan Lawrence, Robert Mead, Derek Rencher, David Drew, Jelko Yuresha, Kenneth Mason, Anthony Dowell, *Maid* Barbara Remington

The version of this ballet now current with the Royal Ballet uses Liszt's music in a different orchestration, by Gordon Jacob

1964—April 2

THE DREAM
(Royal Opera House, for Royal Ballet)

A: after "A Midsummer Night's Dream" by William Shakespeare *D:* Henry Bardon and David Walker *M:* Felix Mendelssohn-Bartholdy *arr:* John Lanchbery

Cast: *Titania* Antoinette Sibley, *Oberon* Anthony Dowell, *Changeling* Alan Bauch, *Puck* Keith Martin, *Bottom* Alexander Grant, *Rustics* Lambert Cox, David Jones, Keith Milland, Ronald Plaisted, Douglas Steuart, with corps de ballet

1965—March 24

MONOTONES
(Royal Opera House, for Royal Ballet)

M: "Trois Gymnopédies" by Erik Satie *orch:* Claude Debussy and Roland Manuel *D:* Frederick Ashton

Cast: Vyvyan Lorrayne, Anthony Dowell, Robert Mead

See below (1966)

1965—December 23

CINDERELLA
(New production—Royal Opera House, for Royal Ballet)

M: Prokofiev *D:* Henry Bardon and David Walker

Cast: Ashton, Helpmann, Grant with *Cinderella* Margot Fonteyn, *Prince* David Blair, *Fairy Godmother* Annette Page, and corps de ballet

See above (1948)

1966—April 25

MONOTONES
(Royal Opera House, for Royal Ballet)

M: (a) "Trois Gnossiennes" by Erik Satie *orch:* John Lanchbery
(b) "Trois Gymnopédies" by Erik Satie *orch:* Claud Debussy and Roland Manuel
D: Frederick Ashton

Cast: (a) Antoinette Sibley, Georgina Parkinson, Brian Shaw,
(b) Lorrayne, Dowell, Mead

See above (1965)

1967—February 10

SINFONIETTA
(Royal Shakespeare Theatre, Stratford-upon-Avon, for Royal Ballet)

M: Malcolm Williamson *D:* Hornsey College of Art Light/Sound Workshop and Peter Rice

Cast: *Toccata* Brenda Last, Kerrison Cooke, Elizabeth Anderton, Richard Farley, *Elegy* Doreen Wells, David Wall, Paul Clarke, Hendrik Davel, Graham Powell, Michael Beare, *Tarantella* Wall, Last, Cooke, Anderton, Farley, with corps de ballet

The same principals were in the cast which first performed this ballet at the Royal Opera House on May 4, 1967

255

1967—December 18

SYLVIA
(New production in one act only—
Royal Opera House, for Royal Ballet)

M: Delibes *D:* R. and C. Ironside

Cast: *Sylvia* Nadia Nerina, *Aminta*
Gary Sherwood, *Eros* Alexander Grant,
Goats Ann Howard, Keith Martin,
Attendants Deanne Bergsma, Monica
Mason, Vyvyan Lorrayne, Christine
Beckley, Rosalind Eyre, Jane
Robinson, Ria Peri, Angele Beveridge,
with corps de ballet

See above (1952)

1968—January 9

JAZZ CALENDAR
(Royal Opera House, for Royal Ballet)

M: Richard Rodney Bennett *D:* Derek
Jarman

Cast: *Monday* Vergie Derman, *Tuesday*
Merle Park, Anthony Dowell, Robert
Mead, *Wednesday* Vyvyan Lorrayne,
Paul Brown, Ian Hamilton, David
Drew, Derek Rencher, *Thursday*
Alexander Grant, *Friday* Antoinette
Sibley, Rudolf Nureyev, *Saturday*
Desmond Doyle, Michael Coleman,
Lambert Cox, Frank Freeman,
Jonathan Kelly, Keith Martin, Kenneth
Mason, Peter O'Brien, Wayne Sleep,
Sunday Marilyn Trounson

1968—October 25

ENIGMA VARIATIONS
(Royal Opera House, for Royal Ballet)

M: Edward Elgar *D:* Julia Trevelyan
Oman

Cast: *Elgar* Derek Rencher, *The Lady*
Svetlana Beriosova, *Steuart-Powell*
Stanley Holden, *Baxter Townshend*
Brian Shaw, *Meath Baker* Alexander
Grant, *Richard Arnold* Robert Mead,
Ysobel Vyvyan Lorrayne, *Troyte*
Anthony Dowell, *Winifred* Georgina
Parkinson, *Nimrod* Desmond Doyle,
Dorabella Antoinette Sibley, *Sinclair*
Wayne Sleep, *Nevinson* Leslie Edwards,
Lady Mary Lygon Deanne Bergsma

1970—February 9

LAMENT OF THE WAVES
(Royal Opera House, for Royal Ballet)

M: "Dans le Deuil des Vagues—II" by
Gérard Masson *D:* Bill Culbert and
Derek Rencher

Cast: Marilyn Trounson, Carl Myers

1970—June 6

THE CREATURES OF PROMETHEUS
(Theater der Stadt, Bonn, for Beethoven
bicentenary celebrations and Royal
Ballet)

M: Beethoven edited by John
Lanchbery *D:* Ottowerner Meyer

Cast: *Prometheus* Hendrik Davel,
Creatures Kerrison Cooke, Doreen
Wells, *Thalia* Alfreda Thorogood,
Terpsichore Brenda Last, with corps
de ballet

CHOREOGRAPHY ADDED TO WORKS IN THE STANDARD REPERTOIRE

THE SLEEPING BEAUTY
(as mounted at the Royal Opera House
by the Sadler's Wells Ballet on
February 20, 1946)

M: Peter Tchaikovsky *D:* Oliver
Messel. *Choreography:* Nicolai
Sergueff after Marius Petipa

ADDITIONS:
February 20, 1946

Garland Dance in Act I
for corps de ballet

Florestan Pas de Trois in Act III
for Michael Somes, Moira Shearer,
Gerd Larsen

January 9, 1952

Aurora's Variation in Act II
for Beryl Grey as Aurora

October 16, 1955

Florimund's Variation in Act III
for Michael Somes as Florimund

Ashton also assisted with the new
production of **THE SLEEPING
BEAUTY**, by Peter Wright with
scenery by Henry Bardon and costumes
by Lila de Nobili and Rostilav
Doubojinsky, which was premièred at
the Royal Opera House by the
Royal Ballet on December 17, 1968.
The cast included Antoinette Sibley,
Donald MacLeary, Deanne Bergsma,
Julia Farron, Merle Park and
Michael Coleman

SWAN LAKE
(as mounted at the Royal Opera House
by the Sadler's Wells Ballet on
December 18, 1952)

M: Peter Tchaikovsky *D:* Leslie Hurry
Choreography: Marius Petipa and
Lev Ivanov

ADDITIONS:

December 18, 1952

Pas de Six in Act I
for Svetlana Beriosova, Alexander
Grant, Rosemary Lindsay, Mary
Drage, Kenneth Melville, Philip
Chatfield

Neapolitan Dance in Act III
for Julia Farron and Alexander Grant

Ashton also assisted with the new
production of **SWAN LAKE**, by
Robert Helpmann with décor by Carl
Toms, which was premièred at the
Royal Opera House by the Royal Ballet
on December 12, 1963. The cast
included Margot Fonteyn, David Blair,
Keith Rosson, Antoinette Sibley,
Merle Park, Brian Shaw and Graham
Usher. For this production Ashton
was responsible for the following
additional choreography:

Prologue

*Waltz, Pas de Quatre and Dance of the
Four Swans, in Act I*

*Dance of the Guests, Spanish Dance
and Neapolitan Dance, in Act II*

Act III (complete)

In this production what had previously
been known as Acts I and II became
Act I, and the whole ballet was
contained within three acts. Currently
(1971) the Royal Ballet has reverted
to a four act version of **SWAN LAKE**
and Ashton's Act III has become
Act IV

September 30, 1960

GISELLE
(as mounted at the Metropolitan Opera
House, New York, for the Royal Ballet
on September 30, 1960)

A: Theophile Gautier after Heinrich
Heine *M:* Adolphe Adam *D:* James
Bailey *Choreography:* Jean Coralli,
Jules Perrot, revised by Nicolai
Sergueff. Additional choreography, and
production, by Frederick Ashton in
collaboration with Tamara Karsavina

Cast: *Giselle* Margot Fonteyn, *Count
Albrecht* Michael Somes, *Berthe* Gerd
Larsen, *Hilarion* Leslie Edwards,
Duke of Courland Derek Rencher,
Princess Julia Farron, *Wilfred* Richard
Farley, *Pas de Deux* Maryon Lane,
Brian Shaw, *Myrtha* Anya Linden,
Zulme Georgina Parkinson, *Moyna*
Christine Beckley

Ashton also made certain additions to
the choreography of **GISELLE** in a new
production at the Royal Opera House
for the Royal Ballet on May 15, 1968.
This production was supervised by
Peter Wright and the scenery and
costumes were by Peter Farmer